Global Political Thinkers

Series Editors
Harmut Behr
School of Geography Politics and Sociology
Newcastle University
Newcastle upon Tyne, UK

Felix Rösch
School of Humanities
Coventry University
Coventry, UK

This Palgrave Pivot series presents ground-breaking, critical perspectives on political theory: titles published in this series present influential political thinkers on a global scale from around the world, with interpretations based on their original languages, providing synoptic views on their works, and written by internationally leading scholars. Individual interpretations emphasize the language and cultural context of political thinkers and of political theory as primary media through which political thoughts and concepts originate and generate. The series invites proposals for new Palgrave Pivot projects by and on authors from all traditions, areas, and cultural contexts. Individual books should be between 25,000 and 50,000 words long according to the Palgrave Pivot format. For more details about Palgrave Pivot, an innovative new publishing format from Palgrave Macmillan, please visit www.palgrave.com/pivot. Emphases shall be on political thinkers who are important for our understanding of:

- the relation between individual and society and conceptualizations of both;
- forms of participation and decision-making;
- conceptualizations of political deliberation and discourse;
- constructions of identity;
- conceptualizations of the 'human condition' of politics;
- ontologies and epistemologies of the political/of politics;
- conceptualizations of social and political change and/or tradition; and
- conceptualizations of political order, their rise and fall.

More information about this series at
http://www.palgrave.com/gp/series/15014

Kevin M. Doak

Tanaka Kōtarō and World Law

Rethinking the Natural Law Outside the West

palgrave
macmillan

Kevin M. Doak
Department of East Asian Languages
and Cultures
Georgetown University
Washington, DC, USA

Global Political Thinkers
ISBN 978-3-030-02034-7 ISBN 978-3-030-02035-4 (eBook)
https://doi.org/10.1007/978-3-030-02035-4

Library of Congress Control Number: 2018957451

This Palgrave Pivot imprint is published by the registered company Springer Nature Switzerland AG
The registered company address is: Gewerbestrasse 11, 6330 Cham, Switzerland

Chief Justice Tanaka Kōtarō, ca. 1954
(permission to reprint from Yuhikaku Publishing Co., Ltd, Tokyo)

Acknowledgements

My research on Tanaka Kōtarō has taken far more time and received far more assistance from other scholars than this slim volume would suggest. I first became aware of Tanaka's *Theory of World Law* at a 1993 academic conference in Milwaukee where Jim Bartholomew introduced it to me. So, of the many people to whom I've become indebted in the subsequent years of my research on Tanaka, it is first and foremost Jim whom I must thank for sparking my interest in the topic. Soon after that, I received a two-volume set of Tanaka's *Zoku sekaihō no riron* from Walter Skya with whom I have had many profitable discussions on Tanaka and modern Japanese jurisprudence since. I was privileged to spend much of summer 2014 in residence at Waseda University as a Global Leadership Program scholar where, under the sponsorship of Uemura Tatsuo and Wakabayashi Yasunobu of the Law Faculty, I was able to study Tanaka's early writings on commercial law. After a series of articles, chapters and presentations on Tanaka for over two decades, it was a sabbatical from Georgetown University and appointment at the International Research Center for Japanese Studies (Nichibunken) in Kyoto during calendar year 2015 that gave me the opportunity to devote myself full-time to my long-held dream of writing a book on Tanaka. I wish to thank my many friends at the Nichibunken, especially Takii Kazuhiro who sponsored me and guided my research on Tanaka during that year. While on sabbatical in Japan, I was greatly assisted in obtaining copies of rare documents at the Tanaka Archives of the Tokyo University Law Faculty by Kokubu Koji to whom I am most grateful. Many people have assisted my research over the years, inviting me to give talks on Tanaka at various universities and professional meetings. There are too many to list here and I'm sure to forget someone. At least I would like to recognize the support and advice I have received from Aida Hirotsugu, Araki Shin'ichirō, Darryl Flaherty, Jieun Han, Hanzawa Takamaro, Makihara Izuru, Kawakubo Tsuyoshi, Jason Morgan, Franklin Rausch, Shibasaki Atsushi, Ko Takemoto, Kei Uno, Mark Williams, and Urs Matthias Zachmann. I also wish to thank Frank Stopa of FSS Photography whose excellent professional skills improved the quality of several of the images used in the book. I also thank Nishino Yasuki of Yuhikaku Publishing Co., Ltd. for permission to use the image of Chief Justice Tanaka that originally appeared in their publication, *Natural Law and World Law: Essays to Commemorate the Sixtieth Birthday of Kotaro Tanaka, LL.D.* (1954) and Yashima Shinji of Misuzu Shobō Publishing Co., Ltd. for permission to use the image of Tanaka in Chapter 3 that originally appeared in their publication, Hanzawa Takamaro, *Kindai nihon no katorishizumu: shisōshi-teki kōsatsu* (1993). I would be remiss not to thank Felix Rösch for his encouragement to submit my work to this series on Global Political Thinkers and to Oliver Foster and Sarah Roughley of Palgrave Macmillan Press for their excellent help in editing my messy manuscript. Finally, my wife Therese and sons Anatole, Emile and daughter-in-law Kelsey have patiently indulged my Tanaka obsession for many years. I hope the publication of this book proves cathartic and provides some respite to them all.

Contents

List of Figures

CHAPTER 1

The Formation of a Japanese Globalist Thinker

Abstract This chapter shows how a number of circumstances in Tanaka Kōtarō's early life prepared him for a life of globalism in culture and thought: frequent relocations during his childhood that exposed him to Japan's varied subcultures and dialects, his years in the all-English language Shūyūkan Middle School laid the foundations for his facility in English, his deep exposure to the globalist humanistic education (*kyōyōshugi*) at the famous First Higher School, his conversion to Christianity, and his extended period of study in Europe from 1919 to 1922. Along the way he engaged deeply with the thinking and writings of Raphael von Koeber, Wilhelm von Kügelgen, and especially Vladimir Solovyov—all of whom were deeply engaged with Christianity. During this period, Tanaka began to think of the law in terms of its moral force rather than as merely a set of technical rules and procedures.

Keywords *kyōyōshugi* · Taisho cultural education · Raphael von Koeber · Wilhelm von Kügelgen · Vladimir Solovyov

Tanaka Kōtarō was born on October 25, 1890 in Kagoshima where his father Tanaka Hideo was employed as a judge. Kagoshima was Hideo's first posting as a judge right after law school. His neighbors threw a big party for him, and his eye fell on a beautiful young girl, the only daughter of the headman of a nearby village, and he soon married Iimori Miku. When Miku gave birth to Kōtarō, one of the friends who came to

K. M. Doak, *Tanaka Kōtarō and World Law*, Global Political Thinkers,
https://doi.org/10.1007/978-3-030-02035-4_1

see the infant was Yamada Saburō (later professor of law at the Imperial University of Tokyo and President of the Japan Academy). Yamada picked up the infant Kōtarō and said, "If I ever become a university professor, I will teach this child" (Tanaka 1961, p. 9). And that is exactly what happened. Yamada looked after young Tanaka from the time he came to Tokyo to study at First Higher School until he graduated from the Imperial University of Tokyo. He also accompanied Tanaka on his first trip to Europe, influenced his theory of world law, and—even at the ripe age of ninety years old—is believed to have influenced Tanaka's election to the International Court of Justice at The Hague. Indeed, Yamada Saburō lived a long life. Born in 1869, he died in 1965, just nine years before Tanaka died. He was a long and consistent globalist influence on Tanaka Kōtarō throughout his life.

Following his father's postings, Kōtarō then moved around the country, living in Nagoya, Matsue, Okayama, Niigata and Fukuoka. Kōtarō's earliest memories were of Nagoya where the family lived from 1892 to 1899, and those memories were suffused with globalist influences. They include the Sino-Japanese War (1894–1895) and the introduction of electric trams. He saw a Chinese prisoner of war in Kenchūji Temple caged like a bird. People came to stare at the prisoner as if he were a circus freak. Tanaka said he never forgot the friendly smile that the Chinese prisoner gave him (Tanaka 1961, p. 10). In 1900 the Tanaka family moved to the remote country town of Matsue. They were only in Matsue for one year, before moving on to Okayama. Tanaka recalled making part of the trip, from Yonago to Tsuyama, by rickshaw. In Okayama, he finished his last year and a half of the prewar system of four years of ordinary elementary school and two years of the higher elementary school and started his first year at Okayama Middle School. Tanaka was a sickly child, but his mother was inspired when she read that Victor Hugo also had been a sickly child but, because of his mother's great care, he lived to be eighty three. Tanaka had to memorize the Confucian classic *On Filial Piety* and his father lectured him on *The Analects* and *Mencius*. In addition to Confucianism, his father was also attracted to Christianity, and referred to the Creator [*zōbutsusha*] and "the God that sees us even if we don't see Him" (Tanaka 1961, p. 12). Tanaka recalled his father as a "progressive," "enlightened" man who enjoyed the company of Christian missionaries. His mother learned Western cooking and introduced it to her friends. He called his parents "pioneers in the rural Movement to Improve Life" (Tanaka 1961, p. 12).

Tanaka moved from Okayama to Niigata and then back home to Kyushu where he was enrolled as a fourth year student in the Shūyūkan Middle School in Fukuoka City. It was a unique school, not only because of its two hundred year history which stretched back to its founding in 1784 by Kuroda Naritaka, a descendant of the Catholic prince Simeon Kuroda Kanbei (Yoshitaka). It was also unique because, decades before Tanaka enrolled, its curriculum already was exclusively conducted in the English language with a heavy emphasis on English and American literature and history. Tanaka was far and away the best student in his class, particularly in English, in large part because his father employed an American missionary to tutor him and Tanaka himself often stayed up all night studying (Abe 2006, p. 16). The fact that Tanaka studied at a rare all-English middle school would prove to be a major factor in his globalism for the rest of his life. In his fifth year of middle school, Tanaka worked hard to prepare for entrance exams to a higher school. He studied English grammar based on the famous Nannichi Tsunetarō's *Method for Interpreting English Composition* (1905). Nannichi, then a professor at Gakushūin University was, along with Kanda Naibu, the leader of English language instruction in the Meiji period and thus one of the early globalist influences in Japanese education.

Yet, because he was a student at a provincial school, Tanaka did not feel confident about his chances of pursuing higher education in Tokyo. At Shūyūkan in his day, there was "Imperial Navy fever" and Tanaka along with his classmates thought the midshipmen at Etajima Naval Academy cut a smart figure with their white jackets and side arms. But there was also a kind of incipient globalism already in Tanaka's thinking: he knew that the Imperial Navy would give him a chance to experience life in a foreign country. He wasn't worried about making the grade academically, but he was worried he wouldn't pass the physical examination. So he applied both to First Higher School and Etajima Naval Academy, with First Higher School as his second choice. His father prepared him for leaving home by citing from *Hamlet* Polonius's words to his son Laertes as he left for France ("Neither a borrower nor a lender be; for loan oft loses both itself and friend, and borrowing dulls the edge of husbandry. This above all: to thine ownself be true, and it must follow, as the night the day, thou canst not then be false to any man"). It does not appear that his father sent spies to keep an eye on his son, as Polonius did. His mother's advice to her parting son was to remember that chastity is not just for women but also important for men. He had already been educated in sexual matters by his father, mainly about venereal disease. But he saw his mother's more spiritual advice as clearly rooted in Christian teaching on the virtue of chastity for both men and women (Tanaka 1961, pp. 16–17). It was not a common idea in the Japan of that time.

In 1908 Tanaka graduated from Shūyūkan Middle School. When studying for the First Higher School entrance exam with former classmates from Niigata and Fukuoka, he had to serve as translator for his friends, given the strength of regional dialects back then. Tanaka said that since he himself didn't speak any dialect—due to his family moving around the country so often—this linguistic fact made him inclined to be a quiet listener rather than a talker. It also encouraged him to think of himself as a cosmopolitan who wasn't completely at home in the Japanese language (Tanaka 1961, p. 13). He was accepted at both Etajima and First Higher School, earning the second highest score on the First Higher School entrance exam. On his father's recommendation, he chose First Higher School. Tanaka saw this moment as an important watershed in his life. He later told his cousin Matsui Keiichi that, had he entered Etajima and become a naval officer, he was certain he would not have enjoyed the success in the military that he had in the law, and at any rate would likely have been killed in the Second World War (Matsui 1975, p. 19). The decision in favor of Japan's most prestigious higher school also took him deeper into the world of cosmopolitan ideas.

In fall of 1908, Tanaka entered First Higher School in Tokyo, specializing in the German Law program. Tanaka reflected that First Higher School, often criticized for being elite or undemocratic, was actually the most successful example of true education in the history of modern Japan. What made First Higher School a special place in his eyes were teachers who taught through art and scholarship the meaning of life and demonstrated it through their own character and cultivated the same in those students who received their personal guidance. Tanaka remembered it as an academic environment where students asked not "what job shall I take when I graduate?" but "what kind of life is worth living?" (Tanaka 1961, pp. 18–19).

The general cultural and intellectual atmosphere of the prewar First Higher School is known in Japanese as *kyōyōshugi*, a term that refers to a particular form of moral culturalism in education that was heavily tinged with globalist culture. A leader in education based on this *kyōyōshugi* was First Higher School's principal, the Christian Nitobe

Inazō. At the welcoming reception for new students, Nitobe told them "not to build walls around themselves but think boldly and work to cultivate their character" (Nitobe Inazō, quoted in Tsutsui 2009; cited in Araki 2012, p. 104.) Tanaka himself was not strongly influenced personally by Nitobe. But he was "deeply moved by the passion of Mr. Nitobe when he lectured on the books he loved so much" (Tanaka 1961, pp. 19–20; also cited in Araki 2012, p. 104). The main intellectual influences on Tanaka during these years were from the famous writers Abe Jirō, Abe Yoshishige, and Uozumi Setsuro (Doak 2011, p. 65). The first two are fairly well-known liberals, both influenced greatly by Western thought and Christianity. Uozumi is less known. His influence on Tanaka can be surmised from the following description of what Uozumi recalled as his personal mission when he was at First Higher School in 1904, just four years earlier: "[I] opposed the vacillating, conservative character of First Higher School and tried to bring in the fresh air of hard work and exercise, standing up for the authority of religion in the non-religious atmosphere of the school" (Uozumi 1977, p. 77; cited in Tsutsui 2009, p. 28). Uozumi was a disciple of Tsunashima Ryōsen who had been baptized in a Protestant Church in Okayama in 1890. In other words, the three greatest intellectual influences on Tanaka during his Higher School years were all deeply suffused with Christian ideas and values.

It is no exaggeration to say that the *kyōyōshugi* that characterized education at the First Higher School was itself very much influenced by Christianity. Christian influence, mainly Protestant, is apparent in the list of intellectual influences Tanaka recalled as shaping the culture of First Higher School when he was there: Raphael von Koeber (the sole Catholic of the bunch), Natsume Sōseki, Tokutomi Roka, Tsunashima, Takayama Chogyū, Uchimura Kanzō, Ebina Danjō, and Chikazumi Jōkan (a Buddhist). There were often lectures on Schopenhauer, Nietzsche and Ibsen. Yet among the students Tanaka recalls in the third year class, those influenced by Catholicism were salient: Iwashita Sōichi (Catholic), Watsuji Tetsurō, Kuki Shūzō (Catholic), Amano Teiyū (Catholic), Tachizawa Tsuyoshi (Nietzsche specialist), Kojima Kikuo (Catholic?) (Tanaka 1961, p. 19). One year behind Tanaka at First Higher School was Totsuka Bunkei who was already Catholic and would later graduate at the head of his class from the Imperial University of Tokyo's Faculty of Medicine (receiving the Imperial Silver Watch as Tanaka did), be ordained a priest, and work together with Tanaka in

Catholic activities before his untimely death from heart failure in 1939. While the influence of Christianity at First Higher School was strong, especially with Nitobe as principle, Iwamoto Tei was one of the most influential teachers of the *kyōyōshugi* movement at First Higher School, and while there is no evidence he had any personal religious faith, his own mentor at the Imperial University of Tokyo had been Raphael von Koeber who had converted from Orthodox Christianity to Catholicism. In Japan, Koeber is considered to be the font of *kyōyōshugi*, suggesting a Catholic foundation to this early twentieth century globalist educational movement (Matsui 1975, p. 22; Takahashi 2005, p. 39).

In his second year at First Higher School, Tanaka came down with typhoid fever. He recovered from the typhus rather quickly. But it left him with a serious case of chronic tuberculous peritonitis. He was immediately taken to his parents' home in Hiroshima, where the doctor pronounced it incurable and gave him less than a year to live. He was told that, even if he somehow managed to survive, his body would never return to full health. He was advised to give up any thought of continuing his rigorous studies at First Higher School and at most consider an easier agricultural school. Desperate, his parents decided to try moxa cautery as a last resort. But each time they lit the moxa, they prayed to God and finally they got an unexpected miracle. The swelling in Tanaka's abdomen starting receding. Thereafter, Tanaka's mother became a firm believer in moxa cautery (Matsui 1975, pp. 27–28). Tanaka, however, became a believer in Christianity. During his five months of recovery, he read Uchimura Kanzō's *How I Became a Christian* and, according to his cousin Matsui Keiichi, he was deeply moved by the lines "only the watchmaker knows the structure of the watch. And only God who created Man knows what Man is" (Matsui 1975, p. 29).[1] This is a very interesting claim, because that line is not found in Uchimura's book. But it was around the same time that Tanaka was also reading Wilhelm Georg A. von Kügelgen's *Jugenderinnerungen eines alten Mannes*, and von Kügelgen made almost the exact same argument for God's existence (see Kügelgen 1871, pp. 57–58). Whether Tanaka imposed his impressions from von Kügelgen onto his memory of Uchimura, or whether his cousin Matsui added this point about the watchmaker analogy is not clear. In either case, it is well-known that Uchimura's book had a decisive influence on Tanaka in his own turn toward the Christian faith. And Christianity in early twentieth century Japan inevitably was linked to globalist culture.

Even so, Tanaka's globalism cannot be reduced to his nascent Christian faith. He later recalled that, of the three globalist Japanese intellectuals who had some influence on him during his years at First Higher School (Nitobe, Uchimura, and Iwamoto), he was most influenced by Iwamoto, the only one who was non-Christian (Tanaka Kōtarō, cited in Yanagisawa 1997, p. 13). Iwamoto is best known as the paradigmatic First Higher School teacher and at the same time the one with the highest standards. His own mentor Koeber influenced Iwamoto to love the classics, especially the Greek classics, and to read them in the original language and absorb everything they offered. Nothing else, including Christianity, mattered to Iwamoto (Takahashi 1993, p. 45). Through this classical education, Iwamoto became committed to a universal search for Truth across time and cultures, and his attitude towards Truth may be best seen from the saying with which he opened his lectures: "Philosophy is the method by which we, with our human limitations, can try to comprehend the cosmos" (Takahashi 1993, p. 114). This belief in a universal truth that can be found through the exercise of reason prepared the ground for Tanaka's later turn toward the Natural Law which in turn was the foundation for his theory of World Law.

As a new student at First Higher School, Tanaka was advised by his senior classmate Tachizawa Tsuyoshi to study German under Iwamoto, so he did (Tanaka, in Yanagisawa 1997, p. 14). Iwamoto made his students read the Great Books of German culture in the original language, regardless of how limited their background in German grammar or syntax was. He also only used imported foreign books, and in class he simply translated the text orally while the students quickly tried to write down in their notebooks every word exactly as he said it (Takahashi 1993, pp. 53–54). The first year, Iwamoto's text was Carl Hilty's *Kranke Seelen* (Sick Souls) which they went through in a semester. Iwamoto's choice of texts was influenced by his mentor Koeber. Tanaka reflected that while he was never taught by Koeber, he felt he was indirectly taught by him through Iwamoto (Tanaka, in Yanagisawa 1997, pp. 14–15).

Around 1910, when Tanaka was in Iwamoto's German class, the text was Wilhelm Georg A. von Kügelgen's *Jugenderinnerungen eines alten Mannes*, von Kügelgen's memories of his youth which were collated and published posthumously by Philip von Nathusius in 1870.

Although hardly known today, the work was immensely popular in *fin de siècle* Germany, and went through 230 editions by 1922.[2] The memoir focuses a good deal on the spiritual life of young Wilhelm, and particularly the tensions between the Protestant faith of his mother and the Catholic faith of his father. Rather than an apologetic work for either form of Christianity, it was oriented toward a transcendence of differences, a sense of Christian unity that was for von Kügelgen a personal, familial matter. Herein may lie the key to its globalist influence on the young Tanaka. It also is a wonderful microcosm of broader social and cultural influences working through rural towns in early nineteenth century Germany—also a point of interest to Tanaka who had lived in several rural Japanese towns. Wilhelm recalls seeing Napoleon riding through his town and how it raised his imagination to a broader new world. Even if read only as the memories of a son who followed in his father Gerhard's work as a painter, the book reflects something of Iwamoto's own globalist cultural values and helps to explain Tanaka's own orientation during his First Higher School years. The work meant so much to Tanaka that he engineered a three volume translation of it, a project that took him and his Higher School classmates Ihara Motoji, Ōsawa Akira and Ueno Isao three years to complete.[3] They began the translation before summer vacation in 1911 and continued working on it even after Tanaka had entered the Imperial University of Tokyo. In 1914, Kōfū Shoin published their translation as *Oitachi no ki* (Records of My Early Life).

The same year, Tanaka took and passed the Higher Civil Service Exam and then graduated from the Imperial University of Tokyo in 1915, receiving the coveted Silver Watch from the Emperor that signaled his standing as one of the very top students at Japan's premier university. After working briefly in the Ministry of the Interior, Tanaka joined the Faculty of Law at his alma mater in 1917. From July 1919 to June 1922, he went to Europe and America as a Ministry of Education Researcher. He left Japan with Professor Yamada Saburō on the Japanese mail ship Fushimi-maru, docking in Seattle. His first impression of America was not positive. He described the country as rent asunder by political ideologies and movements. It seemed to him that ideology had taken the place of careful philosophical reflection among the Americans. Tanaka did not find much reception for his interest in religion and art in the United States (Tanaka 1961, pp. 40–41). After less than two months, he left for England on the RMS Aquitania. In addition to himself and Yamada, another Japanese on board was Kyoto Imperial University professor of international law, Atobe Sadajirō. The conversations they had on board contributed to Tanaka's globalist orientation and were instrumental later in Tanaka's theoretical work on World Law (Tanaka 1961, p. 42).

On arrival in Liverpool, Tanaka was unable to go on to London due to a railway strike, so he spent a bit over a month in Windermere in the northern Lake District. When he finally made it to London, he found it difficult to get lodging because of all the excitement about the Paris Peace Talks. He spent several weeks sleeping on the sofa in Nitobe's flat in London. Nitobe's friend from his Sapporo years, the Christian botanist Miyabe Kingo was there at the time. Nitobe was also at his London home, as the newly-elected Under Secretary General of the League of Nations. Tanaka spent many cold autumn nights with Nitobe, huddling around his stove, discussing Nitobe's interests in Joan of Arc, the topic of luxury, and the philosophy of Plato and Christianity. At one point, Tanaka suggested that politics should be led by religion, only to be upbraided by Nitobe for thinking like Thomas Aquinas (Tanaka, in Yanagisawa 1997, p. 26). Only a few years later, Tanaka was one of Japan's leading Thomists! He recalled this time fondly as his first chance to gain a real intimacy with "the character, thought, culture and everyday life of this great educator, internationalist and patriot [Nitobe]" (Tanaka 1961, pp. 40–41). Tanaka finally secured a room in the house of a woman introduced to him by an Anglican minister, a place not far from Thomas Carlyle's house in the Chelsea district of London. While there, he met the Christian Yoshimoto Tadasu who had married an English woman and devoted his life to the needs of the blind. Tanaka remained good friends with Yoshimoto for the rest of his life.

Overall, however, Tanaka did not care much for England either. He felt that Christianity was dead in the Anglican church, morality had been reduced to an empty formalism, society had ossified, and there was hardly a trace left of the humanism and progress for which England was famous. He even found himself in heated arguments with the dean of his own law faculty, Onozuka Kiheiji, who was in England then, giving talks that struck Tanaka as mere apologies for dead English traditionalism and feudalism (Tanaka 1961, pp. 43–44). And he was disappointed when he finally had the chance to meet the famous Christian writer Tokutomi Roka who was in London on his trip around the world. When Tanaka suggested that the world needed to take down borders and allow people and goods to move freely around the world, Tokutomi told him it was God's will that every ethnic nation (*minzoku*) should live in its own fixed place. Tanaka went home deeply disappointed in this supposed globalist Japanese (Matsui 1975, p. 84).[4]

After but half a year in England, Tanaka crossed over to Paris where his former classmate from First Higher School and fellow translator of Kügelgen, Ōsawa Akira, was waiting for him. It was Easter vacation, so they immediately went to Antibes, France where Ōsawa's landlady Madame Frank had a friend who owned a house. Tanaka spent two weeks in the Côte d'Azur, enjoying the fine weather and French family life. This friend was apparently the only Protestant in the town and his daughter was not shy about giving them a piece of her mind about Catholics (Tanaka himself was still a Protestant at this time) (Tanaka 1948; cited in Suenaga 2005, p. 278). Returning to Paris, he found a small room in the Latin Quarter that overlooked Rodin's The Thinker. While in Paris, Tanaka and Ōsawa also hung out with Ōsawa's Gakushūin University classmate Kōri Torahiko who already had become an established playwright in London. Although Tanaka did not completely share Kōri's classicism, he enjoyed his company. Tanaka recalled finding himself caught between Ōsawa, who liked to spout Marxist jargon, and Kōri, who seemed uninterested in any ideology other than a classicism that sought all answers in art (Tanaka, cited in Suenaga 2005, p. 278). In addition, Ōsawa was obsessed with Romain Rolland and since Tanaka had not read much of Rolland he and Ōsawa found they did not have much to talk about. On the other hand, he was willing to listen to Saitō Hiroshi, a Japanese student in France who encouraged Tanaka to look into Maurice Barrès (Tanaka 1961, p. 46). Barrès at that time had repudiated his earlier anti-semitism and was a spokesman for conservativism and traditionalism in French cultural circles. Tanaka had never heard of him. Tanaka's visit to Verdun only strengthened his own pacifism, as did his discovery that almost everyone he met in France had lost a son in the Great War. Yet, he was struck by how even those who had lost loved ones in the war generally did not share his pacifism. His closest friend during his year in Paris was a student from Kyushu Imperial University named Mori Junjirō with whom he talked about music and art and went on summer jaunts to Belgium, Holland, Germany and Switzerland (Tanaka 1961, p. 48).

Tanaka reflected later that originally his goal on this trip had been to get to Germany since he had studied German since his First Higher School days and particularly because of his work in German law at the Imperial University. One can only imagine how excited he must have been at the prospect of finally seeing Germany, after having lived in Tokyo with the German law professor Theodore Sternberg for two years. But now that he had the chance, he found circumstances had changed. He was no longer in any hurry to get to Germany once he arrived in Paris, as he heard that German feelings toward Japanese were not very warm because they had been enemies during the recent Great War (Tanaka 1961, p. 48). He ended up spending half a year in London, a year in France (seven or eight months in Paris), almost a year in Italy and only three months in Germany (Tanaka, cited in Yanagizawa 1997, p. 153). In addition, from Italy he took a three month trip to Greece, Egypt and Palestine (Tanaka 1961, p. 50). This itinerary, as it turned out, broadened Tanaka's intellectual and cultural interests. Beyond his narrow specialization in commercial law (particularly German theories on commercial law), he was beginning to flourish as a truly globalized young intellectual.

Hanzawa Takamaro has described Tanaka's intellectual orientation during this time as a combination of the three apolitical elements of "a Lutheran sentimental faith, art for art's sake aestheticism, and cosmopolitanism" (Hanzawa 1976, p. 216). Certainly, Tanaka spent much of his time in Europe taking advantage of the Christian, cultural and aesthetic resources he found there. He took piano lessons in London, continued in Paris with his French teacher (a graduate from a Parisian music school) who taught him works by Carl Czerny, and kept at it in Rome where his piano teacher taught him Beethoven's sonatas and works by Muzio Clementi. He played piano for the rest of his life, but never was very skilled at it. Tanaka did not merely learn the piano, but frequently attended concerts, including the London Symphony Orchestra under the direction of Sir Henry Wood. In Rome, Tanaka met the leading critic of legal positivism, Giorgio Del Vecchio of the University of Rome, who remained a good friend for the rest of his life. He also visited Palermo, Naples, Bologna, Ravenna, Verona, Milan, Torino, and Florence. In the end, he had traveled around Italy longer than planned and had to borrow money from his friends to get back to Rome. With his two years coming to an end, and not yet having even been to Germany, Tanaka applied for and received permission to extend his travels for another nine months. He took three of those months and went to Germany. In Berlin, he rekindled his relationships with Sekiguchi Tai,[5] Nasu Shiroshi[6] and Ishikawa Tetsuo.[7] He travelled with Ishikawa to southern Germany and Vienna to hear concerts. He met the Christian composer Nobutoki

Kiyoshi who introduced him to a piano teacher (Tanaka 1961, p. 51).[8] It was also in Berlin where Tanaka took private lessons from the great legal scholar Rudolph Stammler on jurisprudence. He was deeply influenced by Stammler's critique of historical materialism (Tanaka 1961, p. 51).

But it was not merely aesthetics or even jurisprudence that informed his globalism as it matured in Europe. During his stay in Paris, Tanaka was first exposed to the philosophy of Vladimir Solovyov through a biography and anthology of his works put together by Jean-Baptiste Séverac called *Vladimir Solovyov, Les grands philosophes français et étrangers* (Paris: L. Michaud, 1910). Tanaka had chanced on this book which was prominently displayed in a Paris bookstore. He bought it out of curiosity and read it (Tanaka, cited in Yanagisawa 1997, p. 50). Séverac's *Solovyov* appealed to Tanaka for several reasons. His university professor and housemate Theodor Sternberg had already influenced Tanaka to reject legal positivism, and Séverac emphasized one of Solovyov's works called *The Crisis of Western Philosophy: Against the Positivists.* Solovyov, according to Séverac, sought nothing less than to unite religion, philosophy and science in what he called "integrated knowledge" (*savoir intégral*) or "free theosophy" (*libre théosophie*) (Séverac 1910, p. 20). There were obvious, if superficial, intellectual parallels between Solovyov's "free theosophy" and Sternberg's *Freirecht* ("Free Law"), and surely these apparent similarities enticed Tanaka to take a closer look at Solovyov. Solovyov's interest in bridging divides and finding a universal resolution to philosophical and religious differences also mirrored Tanaka's own budding desire to seek a unified field of law which later took shape as his theory of World Law. But in pursuing those possible links, Tanaka encountered something unexpected: Solovyov's religious ecumenism was premised on sharp distinctions between Protestantism, Catholicism and Russian Orthodox Christianity. As Séverac summarized Solovyov's effort at ecumenical unity, he noted that Solovyov ultimately "came to believe that the Orthodox Church was not so superior to the Catholic Church as he had initially thought, and he dreamed of the union of Catholicism and Orthodoxy" (Séverac 1910, p. 28). Tanaka was already aware of the distinction between Protestantism and Catholicism from his study of von Kügelgen, and he personally witnessed the theological, cultural and political struggles that had arisen between Protestants and Catholics in Europe. But whereas von Kügelgen mainly had left these differences at the level of choices various individuals made, Solovyov saw these religious differences as emanating from, or reflected in, philosophical positions with nationalist and globalist cultural implications. He (like Tanaka) was deeply engaged in the pursuit of Universal Truth and was not satisfied with philosophical relativism. While Séverac did not emphasize Solovyov's late conversion to the Catholic Church, he did make it clear that Solovyov was a trenchant critic of modern culture and that his consistent goal was to reconcile culture with religion, specifically with the Christian faith, as an intelligent response to the problems of culture and modernity (Séverac 1910, p. 29). Here, Tanaka found much that resonated with his own intellectual and spiritual quest.

Solovyov's ideas remained with Tanaka throughout his life. And Tanaka's appreciation for Solovyov deepened as he developed his own thinking on law, philosophy and religion over the years.[9] Soon after his return to Tokyo in 1922, Tanaka was asked by Yoshino Sakuzō to substitute for him in giving a lecture at Reverend Uemura Masahisa's Reformed Presbyterian Church in Kōjimachi. Tanaka chose as his topic Solovyov's life and philosophy. Uemura was present, along with Tagawa Daikichi, Professor Saitō Takeshi and Professor Yoshida Seichi who would publish a translation of Solovyov's *The Justification of the Good* five years after hearing Tanaka's lecture. Tanaka was hardly an expert on Solovyov, but was particularly interested in his *Lectures on Godmanhood* (Tanaka, cited in Yanagisawa 1997, p. 50), perhaps because of the globalist orientation of Solovyov's philosophy. As Peter Zouboff has put it, "the realization of Godmanhood implied the universal development of man-godhood" (Zouboff 2007, p. 61). As we saw above, Tanaka had read Séverac's summary of Solovyov's *Lectures on Godmanhood* and it seems highly likely that his lecture was based on Séverac's summary and extracts from *Lectures on Godmanhood*.

Not long after that lecture, Tanaka was asked by Uchimura Kanzō to give another lecture on Christianity at the Eisei Hall, and Tanaka responded with a talk on the problem of salvation called "The Realization of the Law." He drew inspiration from Solovyov's essay on "Nature and Death: Sin, Law and Grace" (included in Séverac's anthology). Solovyov's essay was a meditation on Paul's Epistle to the Romans, particularly chapter seven, where Paul outlines the dualistic nature of Man as following both "the law of God" and "the law of sin." In reflecting on Paul's dilemma (that he does not do what he wants to do but rather does what he does not want to do), Solovyov had concluded that "to the natural suffering that results from our mortal nature is added a moral suffering that results from our internal division (*notre division intérieure*) and from our own condemnation" (Solovyov 1910, p. 88). In his lecture, Tanaka outlined a theory of Man's nature as one of a "dualism" (*nigensei*) between Man's desire to do good and his sinful nature that does evil. This appears to be the source of Tanaka's notion of "Man's dual nature" (*ningen no nigensei*) that Hanzawa Takamaro emphasized in his study of Tanaka's thought, even going so far as to claim that it is the point of departure for Tanaka's jurisprudence (Hanzawa 1993, p. 146).[10] That may be an excessive claim, but there is no doubt that Tanaka was influenced to think in terms of a dualistic structure of human nature by Solovyov's essay on "Nature and Death." Tanaka opened with the contrast between a morality that demands Man improve himself through his own efforts and Christianity that only asks that Man have faith that he has been given the strength to overcome his sins (Tanaka 1922, p. 11). Araki Shin'ichirō sees this lecture as a turning point from Tanaka's youthful acceptance of Nitobe and Iwamoto's facile belief in the perfectability of the person through culture and education. Araki emphasizes that Tanaka still adhered to the Lutheran *sola fide* view of Man's salvation, in line with Uchimura, and that position accounts for the main thrust of Tanaka's lecture on the fulfillment of the law. Araki believes that for Tanaka at this point the State was merely a necessary evil; it had no role to play in the salvation of Man or in his perfection, something which only faith in Christ could accomplish (Araki 2012, pp. 110–111). And indeed, looking back nearly thirty years later, Tanaka described his lecture as "an interpretation of St. Paul's Epistle to the Romans in the manner of Uchimura" (Tanaka, cited in Yanagisawa 1997, p. 42).

Yet, a close comparison of Tanaka's lecture and the growing influence of Solovyov on him reveals there was more to Tanaka's theology than Protestant *sola fide* or even Solovyov's view of Man as a dualistic composite of animal and spiritual desires. Tanaka was also addressing the validity of "the law," by which he also meant a general sense of morality in a pre- or extra-Christian social context, an important consideration for someone like himself who belonged to a largely non-Christian society. Citing Romans 3:21, he argued that "we must recognize that there is a profound meaning even in the law.... The law is the forerunner of faith. Faith will not arise where there is no law... Christ came to us. The world of the law was changed into the world of faith. And the content of the law was changed, deepened and elevated to a place where Man could no longer reach it through his own efforts" (Tanaka 1922, p. 13).

But unlike Solovyov, Tanaka also cited Matthew 5:17–18, "Think not that I have come to abolish the law and the prophets; I have come not to abolish them but to fulfill them. For truly, I say to you, till heaven and earth pass away, not an iota, not a dot, will pass from the law until all is accomplished" (Tanaka 1922, p. 14). And even more to the point, while in most respects Solovyov closely followed St. Paul's Epistle to the Romans, he did not cite Romans 3:31. Tanaka did: "Do we then overthrow the law by this faith? By no means! On the contrary, we uphold the law" (Tanaka 1922, p. 14). Tanaka stressed that faith and works were not in opposition but in fact "the contradiction between them is a superficial, apparent one; in reality, there is no contradiction" (Tanaka 1922, p. 14). He agreed with Solovyov that in our current state we feel the contradiction through our sins. Yet, he also drew from his private lessons in Berlin with Rudolf Stammler on jurisprudence to conclude that love must not be overlooked. Stammler had cited Romans 13:10 ("love is the fulfilling of the law") to emphasize that "religious feeling is indispensable [for justice to prevail]. What we call love in our theoretical discussion comes from religion. Love in this important meaning denotes devotion to the good, to right volition" (Stammler 1923, p. 316). Similarly, Tanaka argued that the resolution to the gap between faith and good works "comes from Christ's love. Christ is love. However, we are able to demonstrate the truth that love is the reconciliation of faith and works through the spirit of love which God has bestowed on us" (Tanaka 1922, p. 15).

Tanaka's conclusion to his lecture echoed the words with which Solovyov had concluded his essay. Tanaka said that

> to believe or not to believe in Christianity… is not a simple matter of culture (*kyōyō/karuchua*) or preference or social improvement. Faith is not a matter of indifference or merely a way to find something better. Faith is not somebody else's problem, but the greatest question that concerns our own life and death. Those who believe will obtain life; those who will not believe are already judged. (Tanaka 1922, p. 16)

Tanaka's lecture was enough in Uchimura's *sola fide* tradition that Uchimura was pleased with it and published it in his journal *Studies in the Bible* later that year. But Tanaka's positive attitude toward the law reveals the influence of his jurisprudence that saw the law not as merely an external coercion, as positivism did, but as reflecting perennial moral truth. This view of "the law" (which certainly came from Stammler but may have also been influenced by Solovyov who held a similar view of the compatibility of secular law and moral law)[11] combined with Tanaka's increasingly evident, critical attitude toward subjectivism and emotionalism, suggests that he was not long for Uchimura's non-denominational Protestant group. It also reminds us that, for all his interest in music, art and other globalist cultural forms, Tanaka was still a highly committed scholar of the law. And his understanding of the law was moving steadily toward a globalist theory of World Law that was rooted in the universal principles of the Natural Law.

Notes

1. Tanaka had to have read Uchimura either in the original English edition or in Luise Oehler's 1904 German translation, as the first Japanese translation did not come out until Ōsaka Shingo's translation of the first three chapters beginning in the November 1910 issue of *Seisho no kenkyū*. The full work did not appear in Japanese until Suzuki Toshirō's publication by Iwanami Shoten in 1935.
2. http://en.wikipedia.org/wiki/Wilhelm_von_Kügelgen. Accessed August 15 2018.
3. Ihara Motoji died in fall of 1918 from a chronic disease and Ueno Isao married Tanaka's younger sister but also had an early death. See Matsui (1975, p. 30).
4. Tokutomi Roka was baptized with his mother in March 1885.
5. Sekiguchi Tai (1889–1956) was a classmate of Tanaka at the Imperial University of Tokyo and later a journalist with the *Asahi* newspaper, postwar chief of the social education bureau of the Ministry of Education, and the first president of Yokohama City University. For more on Sekiguchi's relationship with Tanaka, see below, Chapters 4 and 5.
6. Nasu Shiroshi (1888–1984) was an agriculturalist who graduated from the Imperial University of Tokyo in 1911, and became an assistant professor at the same university in 1917. Later, he served as Minister of Forestry and Agriculture and in the postwar as Prime Minister Yoshida Shigeru's ambassador to India and Nepal.
7. Ishikawa Tetsuo (?–?) was the author of *Ongaku an'gya* (1925), which he dedicated to Tanaka. He later taught German at Fourth Higher School in Kanazawa, and then worked for Ōkawa Shūmei in the East-Asiatic Commercial Intelligence Institute at Tokyo, and later became the Chief of the Research Division of the Home Office of the South Manchurian Railroad. For more on his relationship with Tanaka, see below, Chapter 2.

8. Nobutoki Kiyoshi (1887–1965) was a Japanese composer. He was the son of Presbyterian Pastor Yoshioka Kōki.
9. In 1954, Tanaka published a major essay on Solovyov's jurisprudence that found in Solovyov an important nexus between positive laws and the Natural Law. See Tanaka (1954).
10. Hanzawa's surmising that Tanaka got this idea of "Man's dual nature" (*ningen no nigensei*) from Iwashita Sōichi has influenced some scholars (e.g., Kasuya Tomosuke), including myself in my earlier work (Doak 2011, p. 68). But more recently scholars have shown that Tanaka was using this concept of "Man's dual nature" in his 1922 speech several years before he met Iwashita (Cf. Araki 2012, p. 108; Morikawa 2006, pp. 19–21; Kotani 2011, p. 17). Thus, it appears Tanaka got the idea from Solovyov, not Iwashita. Iwashita refers to dualism (*nigenron*) only in the context of heresy (see Iwashita 1994, pp. 142–143), and describes Man's nature not in dualistic terms but under the two aspects of flesh and spirit (*reiniku no ryōmen*) (see Iwashita 1994, pp. 202–203).
11. For example, Solovyov argued that "we see that the moral ideal fully conforms with the true essence of law. In general, law in its particular character of coercion toward a minimal good, although it does differ from morality in a narrow sense, in no case can contradict it, but even in its coercive character serves the real interest of that same morality." Wozniuk, ed. and trans. (2000, p. 184). See also Séverac, *Vladimir Soloviev*, p. 168.

References

Abe, Noriko. 2006. Shūyūkan no eigo kyōiku: meiji jidai o chūshin ni. In *Ariake kōgyō kōtō senmon gakkō kiyo*, number 42 (July).

Araki, Shin'ichirō. 2005. Tanaka Kōtarō no kyōiku mokutekikan seiritsu: jinkaku no kansei o chūshin ni shite. *Sengo kyōikushi kenkyū* 19 (December): 1–13.

———. 2012. Tanaka Kōtarō no kyōiku mokutekikan seiritsu ni ataeta Jakku Maritan no eikyō. In Nagasaki Junshin Daigaku Katorikku Shakai Fukushi Kenkyūjo, ed., *Katorikku shakai fukushi kenkyū*, vol. 12, pp. 93–151.

Doak, Kevin M. 2011. Tanaka Kotaro and Natural Law. In *Xavier's Legacies: Catholicism in Modern Japanese Culture*, ed. Kevin M. Doak. Vancouver and Toronto: University of British Columbia Press.

Hanzawa, Takamaro. 1976. Shisō keiseiki no Tanaka Kōtarō: chijō ni okeru kami no kuni no tankyū. *Nenpō seijigaku*, 208–240.

———. 1993. *Kindai nihon no katorishizumu: shisōshi-teki kōsatsu*. Tokyo: Misuzu Shobō.

Iwashita, Sōichi. 1994. *Katorikku no shinkō*. Tokyo: Kōdansha.

Kotani, Yumi. 2011. Tanaka Kōtarō ni okeru shizen hō shisō to jinkaku gainen. *Katorikku Kyōiku Kenkyū* 28: 16–29.

Kügelgen, Wilhelm von. 1871. *Bygone Days or, an Old Man's Reminiscences of His Youth*, volume one, translated from the German. London: Chapman and Hall.

Matsui, Keiichi. 1975. *Tanaka Kōtarō hakase*. Saga: Saga Shimbun Sha.

Morikawa, Tamon. 2006. Tanaka Kōtarō no kaishū: Uchimura to no ketsubetsu to 'tasha'. *Nihon shisōshi kenkyū* 38: 17–38.

Séverac, J.B. 1910. Vladimir Soloviev: sa vie et ses écrits. In *Introduction et Choix de Textes Traduits pour la première fois*, ed. J.B. Séverac, trans. Vladimir Soloviev. Paris: Louis Michaud.

Solovyov, Vladimir. 1910. La Nature et la Mort: le Pêché, la Loi et la Grâce. In *Introduction et Choix de Textes Traduits pour la première fois*, ed. J.B. Séverac, trans. Vladimir Soloviev. Paris: Louis Michaud.

Stammler, Rudolf. 1923. Trans. Isaac Husik. The Idea of Justice. *University of Pennsylvania Law Review and American Law Register* 71 (4): 303–317.

Suenaga, Kō. 2005. *Itaria, tabi suru kokoro: taishō kyōyō sedai ga mita toshi to bijutsu*. Tokyo: Seikyūsha.

Takahashi, Kōji. 2005. Inagaki Taruho no katorikku jidai-[Saint] to shinpi shisō. In *Nihon kindai bungaku to shūkyō*, ed. Takitō Mitsuyoshi. Chiba: Chiba Daigaku Daigakuin Shakai Bunka Kagaku Kenkyūjo.

Takahashi, Hideo. 1993. *Idai na kurayami: shi Iwamoto Tei to deshitachi*. Tokyo: Kōdansha.

Tanaka, Kōtarō. 1922. Rippō no jōju. *Seisho no kenkyū* (December): 11–16.

———. 1948. Panteon no yado: ōbei yūgakuchū no omoide 2. *Bungei Shunjū* (November).

———. 1954/1972. Soroviyofu no hō tetsugaku. In *Heiwa no hō tetsugaku*. Tokyo: Yūhikaku; reprinted in Tanaka Kōtarō, *Zoku sekai hō no riron 2*, 501–545. Tokyo: Yūhikaku.

———. 1961. *Watakushi no rirekisho*. Tokyo: Shunjūsha.

Tsutsui, Kiyotada. 2009. *Nihon-gata "kyōyō" no unmei: rekishi shakaigaku-teki kōsatsu*. Tokyo: Iwanami Shoten.

Uozumi, Akio. 1977. *Setsuro shokan shū*. Tokyo: Iwanami Shoten.

Wozniuk, Vladimir, ed. and trans. 2000. *Politics, Law, and Morality: Essays by V.S. Soloviev*. New Haven and London: Yale University Press.

Yanagisawa, Ken. 1997. *Ikite kita michi*. Tokyo: Ōzora Sha.

Zouboff, Peter. 2007. Introduction. In *Lectures on Godmanhood*, ed. Vladimir Solovyov. San Rafael, CA: Semantron.

CHAPTER 2

Law as a Universal Force for Good

Abstract This chapter covers the early years of Tanaka's career as a law professor (1923–1930), a pivotal period when Tanaka got married, converted to Catholicism, and wrote his first book, one of his most important, on *Law, Religion and Social Life* (1927). Building on his discovery of universality in the principles of commercial law, it shows how Tanaka's Christian understanding of the dualism of Man as caught between the flesh and the spirit led him to a broader understanding of law as not a necessary evil but as a social and moral good. In *Law, Religion and Social Life*, he drew on the lessons of President Calles's persecution of Catholics in Mexico to argue that Japanese also must resist efforts to pass laws that would restrict religious freedom, a point he reinforced with references to Pope Pius X's *Vehementer Nos*.

Keywords Commercial law · Religious freedom · World Law
Plutarco Elías Calles · Natural Law · *Vehementer Nos*

One of the key projects Tanaka undertook during the 1920s was an effort to establish commercial law as an autonomous field of law (Inoue 1974, pp. 147–148). At stake was his broader agenda to promote commercial law as a highly globalist field of law in contrast to public law that is more influenced by local mores and values. Tanaka was dissatisfied with previous arguments that defined commercial law merely through narrating its historical development; he astutely pointed out that this

K. M. Doak, *Tanaka Kōtarō and World Law*, Global Political Thinkers,
https://doi.org/10.1007/978-3-030-02035-4_2

traditional narrative was not sufficient as an explanation for the existence of commercial law since narrative approaches in general first assumed the existence of some kind of commercial legal entity in order to narrate it (Tanaka 1923, p. 3). At best, historical approaches merely proceeded from an intuitive understanding of commercial law built up on the basis of a patchwork of case law and "the facts of the cases" (*Tatbestand*). They had not developed a theory of what commercial law in and of itself is. Thus, he concluded, "even today, while we may have theories on the general rules of commercial law, there is still no general theory of commercial law in the true sense" (Tanaka 1923, p. 4). He assessed the theoretical contributions of Karl Wieland's *Handelsrecht* (1921) and especially Victor Ehrenberg's *Handbuch des Gesamten Handelsrechts* (1913), which Tanaka called a breakthrough in understanding the nature of commercial law itself, separate from its manifestations in various particular historical forms (Tanaka 1923, pp. 4–5). Tanaka, following Ehrenberg, rejected as too extreme Philipp Heck's effort to provide a definition of commercial law based on an a priori discovery of the particular character of commercial law in the nature of *Massenbetrieb* (ground operation; mass production; overall working). He concluded that "the study of commercial law needs a general theory in the true sense ... we must be ready and willing to direct our research [toward this question]. If we do not pay attention to this problem, we will have negated from the very outset the existence of commercial law as a field of scholarship" (Tanaka 1923, p. 5). Tanaka noted that commercial law, like procedural law, stood in contrast to fields like family law, inheritance law, and penal law that are deeply colored with moral beliefs that reflect social biases, and that is precisely why he felt commercial law had much to contribute to globalism, not to mention to the resolution of difficult fundamental issues in the study of law itself (Tanaka 1923, p. 7).

Tanaka focused his quest for a theoretical foundation for commercial law in "The Task of Commercial Law" (1924). This is a remarkable article, if for no other reason than it demonstrates, as Inoue Shigeru has pointed out, that Tanaka was more than the abstract theoretician that he is known for being; in this article Tanaka demonstrates his thorough mastery of the positive laws and the technical details of his field (Inoue 1974, p. 167). He referred to particular matters that the Great Kanto Earthquake of September 1923 had raised for private law, particularly the question of whether damages that resulted from the earthquake were covered by insurance or whether the quake should be regarded as an act of God and thus the resulting damages were exempt from considerations of legal responsibility. While he noted that scholars were still debating that point, he emphasized that the answer to that question first required determining what commercial law is, its nature and scope (Tanaka 1924, pp. 60–61).

While other legal scholars sought to define the field of commercial law through adopting new methodologies from the social sciences, Tanaka took a hint from Levin Goldschmidt and argued that it was more important to delve deeper into the basic study of the nature of commercial law than to simply choose a new standpoint (*neuer Standpunkt*) from which to look at commercial law (Tanaka 1924, pp. 26–27). Once again, he held that it was first essential to know what one was looking at before deciding on a lens through which to view it. Deep in history, Tanaka found that in the medieval period Christianity had played an important role in the formation of commercial law, particularly through the Catholic Church's teaching against usury. This was not merely a "cultural curiosity" but evidence of "a metaphysical contemplation on the relationship of religion to law" (Tanaka 1924, p. 24). His own professor and house-mate Theodor Sternberg had taught him that Greek legal philosophy had focused on the State and that Roman jurisprudence had developed private law, but that legal studies from the medieval period onwards had built on the Christian theme of sin and atonement, finding its real home in criminal law.[1] Later injections of Christian and communitarian elements in the secular, individualistic field of commercial law created tensions that had been left unresolved. But from the middle to late nineteenth century, the fusion of Roman, German, and modern elements within commercial law had created "the first step toward globalism" (*sekaishugi no daiippo*) within the legal field (Tanaka 1924, p. 26). Still there only remained mountains of facts and methods; what was lacking was "a unified, comprehensive study of commercial law" (Tanaka 1924, p. 27). Tanaka believed that by establishing such a general theory of commercial law, jurists could move the field of law even deeper into globalism.

As an example of the possibility of a unified understanding of the field of commercial law, Tanaka presented his own hypothesis. To define the nature of commercial law it was necessary, he believed, to take seriously the ordinary facts of life that commercial law regulates. When the law is understood as the means or form of social life, the kind of life that is the material of a particular legal field determines the nature of those means and forms. Thus, he concluded, research into the nature of commercial law must take as its point of departure the actual facts of life that form its foundation (Tanaka 1924, p. 37). These actual facts of life are, in a word, the economy. And if the economy can be seen as a coherent field of study, as economists maintain, then drawing on their logic, commercial law could also be established as a coherent field of law. Tanaka introduced his provocative theory on the identification of commercial law as a special field of law, separate from other areas of private law, in the following terms:

> I believe one can, without inquiring into the type of legal facts, distinguish between private and commercial law on the basis of whether the legal facts of a general private law nature have a commercial coloring or not (*shōteki ni chakushoku saretari ya ina ya*). One must say that, in contrast to the distinctions among various legal fields that have been made previously, the opposition of private and commercial law constitutes a certain peculiar relationship. It is different from the contrast between private, criminal and procedural law, but rather similar to the relationship of constitutional and administrative law. I want to set forth the proposition that commercial law is a separate field of law from private law and enjoys an exceptional position in law through the logic of the coloring (*Tönung*) of otherwise identical legal facts. (Tanaka 1924, p. 43)

Consequently, Tanaka concluded that the most important task confronting commercial law was to study how general concepts of private law may have taken on a teleological coloring (*mokutekironteki ni chakushoku serarete iru*) through trade (Tanaka 1924, p. 44). The key to discovering a unitary field of commercial law was this element of teleology or purpose. By identifying a common purpose among individuals engaged in a commercial transaction, Tanaka felt that one could find unity in a field of law, in spite of various differences in the positive laws related to that field (Tanaka 1924, p. 54).

Another important point for Tanaka was that, in contrast to both private law and criminal law which are both commonsensical and ethical, commercial law is specialized and ethically amoral (Tanaka 1924, p. 49). The moral norms or particular forms of common sense that delineated criminal law within a particular society or culture, for example, contrasted with the technical norms of commercial law that made the latter field more capable of describing legal rules for all people in commerce, regardless of their cultures or moral traditions. Violations of rights in civil affairs are often seen as attacks on the person, whereas in commercial law, violations are less personal and more often the result of weighing rational interests. This aspect makes it easier to reconcile opposing parties in commercial law cases than in other kinds of legal cases (Tanaka 1924, pp. 49–50). But this technical, "amoral" nature of commercial law does not mean that it has no moral implication in practice. Tanaka noted that the subject of commercial legal studies already extends beyond the realm of pure law to include relations that are within the scope of economics and sociology, and so by the same standard he concluded that relations in spiritual matters could not be excluded from consideration. "So long as the phenomena of commercial law constitute a part of legal life they will necessarily also touch on the spiritual life of Man. And that may require us to look at the relation of law to morality and religion" (Tanaka 1924, pp. 62–63). That is precisely what Tanaka did in his first book, *Law, Religion and Social Life* (1927).

Even as Tanaka was working on a theory of commercial law, another momentous event took place in his own spiritual life that had a decisive influence on his globalism. This event was his break with Uchimura Kanzō, his spiritual counselor. The immediate cause was a fight in April 1924 over whether Ishikawa Tetsuo could marry a certain Mrs. K. Both were members of Uchimura's "non-Church" Christian circle, and Tanaka had become a close friend of Ishikawa while they were in Berlin together. Ishikawa's first wife had died and he had since fallen in love with Mrs. K, the wife of Ishikawa's friend, a diplomat who had been posted overseas for a long time. There were rumors that Mr. K was having relations with lots of women overseas, and at any rate he had treated his wife coldly for quite some time. On top of that, there were religious differences between the husband and wife. Tanaka was quietly sympathetic to Ishikawa and Mrs. K's plight. As their circle, all disciples of Uchimura, started criticizing the couple for their immoral life together, Tanaka's sympathy for them only grew stronger. Uchimura held that the Bible clearly stated that marriage is indissoluble and to remarry would be an act of adultery. He strongly forbade the proposed marriage between Ishikawa and Mrs. K and in fact excommunicated the two from his circle. This meant that they were socially ostracized. Tanaka, however, saw the matter differently and he was not about to abandon his friends. He argued that Mrs. K's first marriage was a sham, utterly without love, and as such it could not be considered a legitimate marriage. Moreover, her first husband was supportive of the new marriage proposal and had legally divorced her. Tanaka could find no reason the two should not be married, and he stressed that Christianity, a religion of love, could not be used against this marriage when the two were clearly in love and there was no legal impediment to their marriage. Uchimura had refused an invitation to attend the wedding as the couple's official matchmaker, so Tanaka agreed to do so, and for that act of rebellion Uchimura excommunicated him, too. The rift was permanent. It was a painful lesson for Tanaka, but an essential one for his move towards embracing a universal authority that would lay the foundations for his theory of World Law. He also learned a lesson about the arbitrariness of the authority of a charismatic individual (Uchimura), a lesson that paved the way for his embrace of the authority of impersonal, global institutions.

Ishikawa Tetsuo had a greater personal impact on Tanaka than the marriage debate alone might suggest. Shortly after Tanaka had been excommunicated by Uchimura, Ishikawa introduced Tanaka to Matsumoto Mineko. Ishikawa had worked for her father Matsumoto Jōji in the South Manchurian Railway and had known Matsumoto's in-laws, the Koizumi family, since childhood as they were neighbors in the Mita district of Tokyo. Tanaka was soon engaged to Mineko who was also Christian. However, as Tanaka recalled, there was still a religious problem: Mineko was Anglican, as was her mother, but her father (Tanaka's former professor) was not enthusiastic about Christianity at all, nor was he enthusiastic about having his former student Tanaka as his son-in-law. In addition, Mineko was already thinking of converting to Catholicism, but she had stayed Anglican out of respect for her mother's feelings. Tanaka was still a non-denominational Christian and would make no promises about converting to either Anglicanism or Catholicism as a condition of marriage (Tanaka 1961, p. 57). Nonetheless, in July 1924, Tanaka married Mineko and they lived for next three years in Abiko, Chiba with many other refugees from the Great Kanto Earthquake. Six months later, in January 1925, Mineko joined the Catholic Church. Tanaka, however, did not immediately follow suit. It was not until the Easter Vigil Mass on April 3, 1926 that Tanaka joined Mineko as a Catholic. His godfather was one of the great globalist intellectuals of modern Japan, Fr. Iwashita Sōichi, who had recently returned from six years of study in Europe.

As Tanaka was preparing to join the Catholic Church, he was also writing his first book, *Law, Religion and Social Life*, which was also one of his most important books. Tanaka himself said that this book "may be called my conversion to Catholicism book" (Tanaka 1961, p. 59). Hence it is not surprising that much of the scholarly discussion of *Law, Religion and Social Life* has centered on it being an expression of Tanaka's newly-found Catholic faith. Hanzawa sees it rather as indicative of Tanaka's residual Protestantism, "giving us the image of a Lutheran Tanaka" (Hanzawa 1993, p. 131). Others who do accept *Law, Religion and Social Life* as an authentic expression of Tanaka's Catholic faith share Hanzawa's emphasis on the role of the concept of "Man's dual nature" (*ningen no nigensei*) as central to the work (Kasuya 1999; Araki 2012; Kotani 2011).[2] But in fact, Tanaka mainly brought up the concept of "Man's dual nature" (which, as we saw in Chapter 1, he had broached several years earlier in his lecture to Uchimura's group) in one section of the book's third chapter where he discussed the relationship of law and religion. His point was that religion and law have different functions and should not be confused. In religion, in spite of the necessity of upholding the moral law, no one was able to do so perfectly. In law, however, even an ordinary person is capable of observing the civil law, even if sometimes the most intelligent and capable people choose to violate the law (Tanaka 1927a, pp. 32–42). In contrast to his 1922 speech on St. Paul's complaint about the impossibility of perfectly upholding the moral law, Tanaka's point now was less about moral philosophy than about the relationship of law to religion. He only introduced the earlier idea of "Man's dual nature" to make an analogous point about the irreducibility of religion to politics and law.

Tanaka stated in the opening pages what motivated him to write *Law, Religion and Social Life*:

> A draft Bill on Religion which has been of concern for some time has recently been announced and a committee has been composed of government officials, legal scholars, and experts in religion. Serious deliberations on what should be in the Bill already have begun, and these developments have attracted the attention of the intelligentsia. A basic understanding of the relationship of the law to religion has now become essential … This is what I would like to take up in this book. (Tanaka 1927a, pp. 5–6)

Tanaka then quickly added that "it is not my purpose to evaluate the Bill on Religion. Evaluations of the details of the Bill have already been published in many quarters and I believe they will continue in the future so I will refrain from doing so now. Here, I merely want to discuss the fundamental relationship of law and religion which is merely one very small part of the Bill on Religion. If in doing so, indirectly attention is drawn to the intellectual background that has led to this Bill on Religion, nothing would make me happier" (Tanaka 1927a, pp. 6–7). One should not misread this statement as discounting the importance of the Bill on Religion as motivation for Tanaka to write this book. Far from it. Tanaka's language is merely that of a careful legal scholar who wished to avoid polemics and get to the heart of the fundamental questions that ought to inform the relationship of law to religion.

Tanaka was responding in part to events that began on May 5, 1926 when Minister of Education Okada Ryōhei of the Wakatsuki Cabinet announced the formation of a Research Committee on Religious Institutions that would be attached to the Ministry of Education. Its main function was to investigate and deliberate on questions posed by the Minister of Education regarding the Bill on Religion. From June to August, the Research Committee discussed the Bill that had been drafted in the Religion Division of the Ministry and suggested some revisions to it. The revised Bill was submitted to the House of Peers in January 1927, one month after Tanaka finished writing *Law, Religion and Social Life*. Ultimately, the Bill did not pass due to strong opposition, and Tanaka's book was certainly a factor in shoring up the opposition. Another effort was made in 1929 but it too failed in the House of Peers. It was not until 1939 that the Religious Organization Law was passed, going into effect April 1, 1940. In the context of wartime Japan, the debate over the Bill on Religion was often seen as pitting globalists against nationalists, especially Shintoists. And Tanaka was a leading voice among Japanese globalists.

But Tanaka's concerns were not limited to Japan. His conversion to Catholicism heightened his awareness of the fraught relationship of religion and politics in the early twentieth century, particularly the persecution of Catholics around the world. As he brought up in *Law, Religion and Social Life*, there were two main issues that had direct bearing on the religious freedom of Catholics even in places where historically Catholics were the majority, not the religious minority they were in Japan. First, he cited from Pope Pius X's encyclical *Vehementer Nos* evidence of a global retreat from the fundamental principle of international law that "treaties must be obeyed" (*pacta sunt servanda*).

Pius X had issued *Vehementer Nos* in 1905 as a protest against the unilateral abrogation by the French government of the Concordat it had signed with the Vatican. In his book, Tanaka cited from *Vehementer Nos* the following line: "The Concordat entered upon by the Sovereign Pontiff and the French Government was, like all treaties of the same kind concluded between States, a bilateral contract binding on both parties to it" (Pius X 1906; cited in Tanaka 1927a, p. 178.) Pope Pius went on to say, in the most famous (and most infamously misrepresented) line of the encyclical, "that the State must be separated from the Church is a thesis absolutely false, a most pernicious error" (Pius X 1906.)[3] The cause and effect of the laicization movement in France that led to the unilateral abrogation of the treaty ("Concordat") with the Vatican was a rise in anti-religious ideology that was depriving French citizens of the full exercise of their religious freedom, as Pius X bemoaned.

The other example of a seriously mishandled relationship of law to religion was more dramatic. On November 18, 1926, Pius XI issued the encyclical *Iniquis Afflictisque* that decried the violent persecution of Catholics in Mexico. While the 1917 Constitution of Mexico had laid the ground for this persecution with a number of oppressive laws that effectively subordinated the Church to the State, the immediate spark was the 1924 election of the aggressively atheist Plutarco Elías Calles to the presidency, and his vigorous enforcement of the constitutional restrictions on religious life and the enactment of the even more draconian "Calles laws" that effectively shut down all Church activities in Mexico. What followed was the Cristero Wars that by 1929 would claim more than 90,000 lives. Tanaka listed in detail the various laws that were used to oppress Catholics in Mexico, and his point was that the law could be used to oppress religious rights (Mexico) or the law could be violated in pursuit of the same goal (France). And if the religious rights of Catholics could be denied in majority Catholic countries, what guarantee was there that any Japanese person, whether minority Christian or majority Shinto/Buddhist, could rest secure in the belief that it could not happen in Japan? Tanaka's recommendation was, perhaps, a surprising one:

> What we can see from the above examples is that we must recognize that the separation of State and religion is the religious policy that we should choose. But this must not be a separation based on a materialist world view as in Soviet Russia, or based on the principle of antagonism to religion that one sees in France or Mexico. Rather it is the separation as practiced in

> the United States of America which has an understanding of religion as a whole and is motivated by good will toward religion and treats all religions equitably. (Tanaka 1927a, p. 173)

Tanaka was not advocating a wholesale Japanese incorporation of American laws concerning religious freedom so much as he was pointing to historical examples where religious freedom was more, rather than less, well protected.

The lesson Tanaka drew from these cases of religious oppression is that it was essential for Japan to get the legal relationship between the State and religion right. He presented three models from world history of efforts to solve this problem: (1) the idea that the State should determine one religion for all its members (caesaropapism); (2) the idea that Church and State are completely independent, a position common to the Soviet, Mexican, French and American models, but which takes the Church as no more than a juridical person or public interest corporation that can be regulated as the State wishes; and (3) a syncretic approach such as in Germany where all religious organizations are accorded special treatment as social organizations with special privileges, although the State retains the right to meddle in internal affairs of these special organizations to a greater degree than with other private corporations (for example, in the appointment of clerics, establishing compensation and the like) (Tanaka 1927a, pp. 114–117). Tanaka identified Japan's position under the Meiji Constitution as a combination of the first (caesaropapism) and the second (secularism). Caesaropapism and secularism combined in the Japanese government's position that all Japanese should visit Shinto shrines to show their respect and that this requirement does not violate the constitutional principle of religious freedom because "shrines are not religious" (*jinja wa shūkyō ni arazu*). Tanaka was quick to notice that if Shinto were deemed not a religion, then the Bill on Religion would not apply to it, and he pointed out that this would put other religions at a comparative disadvantage. Therefore, he concluded that, while recognizing that arriving at an ultimate determination as to whether something is a religion or not is difficult, a commonsense standard can and should be applied to the question. The commonsense standard he offered was that "matters dealing with a Being greater than Man and our relationship to that Being must be considered religious" (Tanaka 1927a, p. 123). By that standard, Shinto is a religion and, as such, it must fall under the Bill on Religion. Not to do so would be to pull an end-run around the law.

Tanaka concluded that the Japanese State had only two options: either shrines must be prohibited from engaging in any religious activity or they must be recognized as religious organizations and fall under the scope of the Bill on Religion (Tanaka 1927a, pp. 126–127). It should also be noted that Tanaka did not exempt Yasukuni Shrine from "true Shinto" by arguing that it was a political institution, as some have more recently held. In fact, his argument that Shinto was a religion was primarily concerned with the Yasukuni Shrine which had been the centerpiece of the government's argument that "shrines are not religious." Tanaka was fully cognizant of the dangers of politicians and others determining which specific religious practices are authentically religious and which are not. The key principle guiding his thinking is what today is often called "religious tolerance." But Tanaka made an interesting distinction concerning religious tolerance. He argued strongly that the State must practice political tolerance (*bürgerliche Toleranz*) which he defined as adopting a policy that recognizes the equality (*Parität/byōdō*) of all religions. But he did not say that government must be secular in the sense that every government must be completely free from any religious identification, regardless of its cultural or historical background. Such "a mechanical equality" would not be of help in the State achieving its purpose [the human flourishing of the people in its jurisdiction]. He held that it was only a matter of justice that the State take into consideration various religions' historical and social contributions to a particular society (Tanaka 1927a, pp. 161–162). At first glance, this position might seem to contradict his argument that Shinto shrines should not enjoy legal privileges over other religions. But it was no contradiction. What Tanaka was arguing for was a vibrant Shintoism that took its place in Japanese society alongside other religions, and he was not prepared to deny Shinto's many contributions to Japanese history and culture. He simply wanted the religious identity of Shinto to be acknowledged and the rigorous secularism of those who denied Shinto to be a religion to be checked.

On this point, Tanaka was likely influenced by Pius X's words in *Vehementer Nos*: "that the State must be separated from the Church is a thesis absolutely false, a most pernicious error. Based, as it is, on the principle that the State must not recognize any religious cult, it is in the first place guilty of a great injustice to God" (Pius X 1906). But Tanaka made it clear that this argument must not be used to promote only one religion: "Take, for instance, a case where a government is composed of members of a certain religion (for example, Catholicism). In this case, the government must observe tolerance in the political sense (*bürgerliche Toleranz*). When believers of a certain religion are the rulers, they are not allowed to do anything like protecting their own religion while oppressing other religions, and in this sense, political tolerance must be sharply distinguished from religious tolerance (*religiöse Toleranz*) (the latter is indifferentism, which is unacceptable)" (Tanaka 1927a, p. 160). Tanaka's parenthetical remark is telling. He felt strongly that it is the role of the State to provide a neutral forum for religious debate and that it is the obligation of all people to express their beliefs in public and to try to convince others, through reason, of their own religious position. So long as all are accorded this right, he found no ground for concern over religious oppression. He was of course acutely aware of the tensions between a neutral State, in this sense, and a secular State that has no religious coloring (which he, along with Pope Pius X, felt was also unjust). And he dealt with this tension broadly with reference to his general point that the law is not perfect, but is engaged in a constant compromise (*Kompromissnatur des Rechts*) that ever seeks a more perfect resolution to those conflicts inherent in society (Tanaka 1927a, p. 196).

If the law is characterized by the nature of compromise, there must be a principle that transcends society and which can be used to measure whether a social solution is indeed a compromise. If not, the "compromise" is merely an open-ended question that ultimately rests on a final resolution through power. Tanaka believed that if the law were to be more than a justification of the position of those in power, if it were to possess a critical function of its own, then the law required this transcendent principle from which one could measure progress in achieving fair and equitable resolutions of conflict. Thus, toward the end of *Law, Religion and Social Life*, he introduced "the problem of World Law" to explore the possibility of identifying such a trans-national standard of judgment. Once again, Tanaka drew a fine line between two extremes: those who make a utopian leap directly to World Law or a Unified Law while ignoring those aspects of the law that are relative to social conditions ("*la relativité de droit*") and those who hold that the law was completely relative, nothing more that a product of ethnic national history, and who relished the differences among laws as signs of ethnic national differences. His effort to find a middle ground between these two extremes is worth quoting:

> Among cultural phenomena, there are those things like literature, philosophy and art that speak to all mankind but at the same time reflect the individuality or even the national characteristics (*kokumin no tokusei*) of the writer, scholar or artist, and those things too have a certain nobility to them. But conversely there are also in fact things which have an ethnic coloring but whose nature does not require respect for those ethnic elements, or like science and technology completely transcend national borders and ethnicity. I cannot agree with the attitude adopted by scholars of a certain school who oppose World Law while giving too much weight to historical or natural differences based on ethnic nationality. (Tanaka 1927a, pp. 210–211)

Tanaka then focused on the move toward unification in law that was then growing in strength around the world, referring specifically to Ernst Zitelmann's seminal 1888 lecture given in Vienna on "Die Möglichkeit eines Weltrechts" (the possibility of a World Law). While Tanaka cited Zitelmann's belief that major moral norms among people in the world were converging, his main emphasis was on those areas of law, particularly commercial law, that were largely morally neutral (for example, "on which side of the road should one drive?") and which were most determined by their goal-oriented nature or purposefulness (*Zweckmässigkeit*).

But technique alone cannot answer for its choice of purpose or *telos*, and for that Tanaka pointed to the need for a method of establishing priorities among conflicting goals, which was, simply put, the matter of justice (*Gerechtigkeit*). Is it possible that laws based on a concept of justice might also reach some level of unity across cultures? Here, Tanaka followed Zitelmann in rejecting, as a "forced argument," the effort to defend moral relativism by "fictitious strange tales" (*gisei-teki chindan*) like saying that "in Sparta theft was encouraged" or "when certain barbarians are asked what is right and wrong they answer that it is right when I take someone else's wife and wrong when someone takes my wife." While conceding there are cultural differences in matters like table manners, he argued that "moral ideals that form the basis of legal norms necessary to social life are given to Man by his nature and are commonsense throughout the world. In this sense, one can recognize the possibility of unity even in laws of a moral nature" (Tanaka 1927a, pp. 225–226).

Tanaka's rebuff to moral relativists is worthy of note. But he did not maintain that this unity of laws, particular those dealing with matters of justice, already had been realized. Rather, he said, "I do not believe it will be possible to have unity in all areas of law or that such possibility has the same strength in all areas of law. As I have repeatedly stressed, law follows actual social life and in that sense is something relative. Law differs from morality or religion in that it has a great many elements based on facticity (*jijitsusei*) which is to say, elements that are customary" (Tanaka 1927a, pp. 226–227; emphasis in original). In spite of those areas of cultural difference where a unification of laws was less likely, or even undesirable, Tanaka held that an effort at building a field of universal World Law was not only important, but indeed was required by the times. Yet, he was not a starry-eyed idealist. In fact, he staked out a rather modest claim to World Law:

> I am not like those *Weltrechtler* that the world ridicules for dreaming that the laws of the world can be unified everywhere. I critically distinguish where the laws can be unified and where they cannot, and try to unify laws where it is rational and appropriate to get rid of unreasonable difference in national laws that create inconvenience, in step with the ideals and movements of various nations … The reason we have not made as much progress in unification of laws as we should is because of national prejudice that keeps some scholars clinging to their own legal principles and traditions.
>
> I am neither a World Law optimist nor a World Law denier … The question is one of principle: should law be regarded as something that is humanistic and universal, or something particular that cannot escape historical national factors? I favor the theory of unification from the position that we should more heavily appraise the ideal nature of law in the competition between the ideals and the facticity of law, and I do believe that Man's rational nature and concepts of justice in the end can be reconciled into one. (Tanaka 1927a, pp. 228–230)

Tanaka's position in favor of World Law drew from Rudolf Stammler and other German scholars who took a sociological approach to law and separated the question of law from that of political sovereignty and the State. Law comes not from the State, Tanaka argued, but from society. And there were not only many types of particular societies (corporations, churches, private associations), but he also pointed to the existence of many world societies in the sense of organizations formed around specific goals that transcended national boundaries. Against those who argued there can be no world law without a world court, Tanaka pointed out that the existence of substantive law is not contingent on the ability to enforce the law. That kind of argument merely severs law from its intimate relationship to society and takes one back to John Austin's command theory of sovereignty or to legal positivism. Rather, Tanaka proposed the way to establish World Law was to liberate the content of law from ethnic nationality (*minzokusei*) and the form of law from the sovereignty of the State (*kokka shuken*) (Tanaka 1927a, pp. 234–235).

To separate law from the State (or from sovereignty), or indeed from any historically reductive understanding of the law, required an understanding of what law in general is, that is, the nature of law as an ideal. He illustrated the idea that law is not merely the sovereign's will by referring to the classic maxim *ubi societas ibi ius* (wherever there is society, there is law) (Tanaka 1927a, pp. 85–86).[4] It was a maxim he would return to often in his writings. But here he simply showed how this idea emerged from a recognition that the Catholic Church, as a "society," had its own laws, and thus law could not be reduced to the political agency of States and sovereigns. If law did not stem from sovereignty, then what was its source?

To answer that question, Tanaka introduced the idea of the Natural Law. He was fully aware that positivists would reject his argument for the Natural Law and argue instead that the content of Natural Law claims are determined by particular historical conditions. Tanaka conceded that the Natural Law took on various forms throughout history, but he pointed out that this fact itself was proof that there must be something behind those historical forms that kept returning the question of the Natural Law to jurisprudence across different historical periods and cultures. He shared with positivists and historicists a rejection of the Natural Law of Enlightenment Rationalism that considered subjective decisions by legislators or judges or scholars as ipso facto rational and thus universal. Nor was he swayed by Natural Law theories derived from psychological studies of human nature. He insisted, however, that the idea (*rinen*) of law must be sought in an order above law itself,[5] that is, in the world order that was designed by God's reason. Tanaka was quite candid about the fact that his own interest in the Natural Law was relatively new and there were still many questions he had not answered. So, he concluded by promising to develop this argument on the Natural Law through subsequent study of St. Thomas Aquinas's "Lex Aeterna" (Tanaka 1927a, pp. 238–240).

It is important to recognize that Tanaka did not come to the Natural Law from abstract philosophical or theological speculation, but from concrete problems in the field of law, particularly in private international law. Only then did he consider philosophical arguments for Natural Law like those of St. Thomas Aquinas. He drew from Rudolf Stammler's invitation to place law in a social context, and he concluded that those concerned with the law faced an inevitable choice: "we will come to different conclusions based on whether we see law centered on the sovereignty of the state or an ethnic nation, or whether we see law as centered on human society" (Tanaka 1927a, p. 246). Tanaka left no question as to how he answered the question himself. He saw law as centered on society as a global phenomenon.

A brief review of the critics of *Law, Religion and Social Life* may help to situate Tanaka within the struggles for globalism in early twentieth century Japan. Those critics came mainly from three positions: Shintoism, Marxism and Buddhism. Minoda Muneki has often been described as an anti-communist ideologue (which he was), but that hardly captures his role in prewar Japan. He and his organization, the Genri Nihonsha, were generally against any form of universalism, but Minoda had a particular agenda against Christianity which extended even to Christians like Tanaka who shared his opposition to communism.[6] From his ethnic nationalist Shintoist perspective, Minoda argued that Tanaka's dualistic thinking on Church and State was itself relative, merely a product of Western culture, and showed his "general lack of research in ethno-national psychology and cultural history, particularly a lack of understanding and study of the special nature of the Japanese State and the religious faith of the Japanese" (Minoda 1927, pp. 26–28). Ironically, while Minoda tried to relativize Tanaka's universalism, he universalized his own ethnic nationalism, finding it everywhere in the Mid-East ("Jesus was an ethnic nationalist") and Europe and blaming imperialism (the Roman Catholic Church) for suppressing this natural ethnic nationalism in Europe and elsewhere.

A Marxist critic, identified only by the initials M.K., also rejected Tanaka's idea that Christianity could offer a universal principle from which to criticize politics, arguing that all religion was merely a social product and, as such, Tanaka's Christian faith marginalized him in Japanese society. M.K. insisted only "proletarian science" could change society for the better (M.K. 1927, p. 3), although he seemed oblivious to the irony that proletarian science was also a social product of the West and even more socially marginalized in Japan than Tanaka's Christianity was. Tanaka wrote a polite but effective reply to M.K. at the insistence of the editors of the *Imperial University Newspaper*. He was startled to find M.K. misreading him so badly as to conclude Tanaka was glorifying the current Japanese State. "A strong dissatisfaction with the existing State and society is a recurring basic theme of the whole book," he exclaimed, and he pointed to his discussion of the Yasukuni Shrine issue as evidence (Tanaka 1927b, p. 3).

Tanaka's third critic was his own Imperial University of Tokyo Law Faculty colleague Ono Seiichirō who launched a Buddhist attack on him.[7] Like Minoda, Ono argued that Tanaka gave the Church too much legal independence from the State; ultimately, he concluded that Tanaka's arguments cannot be theoretically reconciled with the sovereignty of the State. "This kind of duality that insists that the law of the State and the law of the Church are mutually independent in their validity, even within the same territory, is something I am thoroughly opposed to" (Ono 1927, p. 74). He added that Tanaka's dualism reflected an unforgivable presumption that material life is merely the slave of the spiritual life. Ono concluded by saying that Tanaka's "heretical view" (*jaken*) is of a type that is injurious to an authentic spiritual life, and he doubts he could live with a legal thinker of Tanaka's religious views without compromising his own values (Ono 1927, pp. 74–75). Tanaka responded to Ono's criticisms in detail, and he noted that Ono's rejection of Canon Law as a legitimate form of law would not be of much value in opposing the Bill on Religion which also threatened the position of Buddhists. He concluded on a strong note that "your last words [about not wanting to live with someone of Tanaka's religious views] shows us what your attitude toward scholarship really is" (Tanaka 1927b, p. 3).

Of Tanaka's critics, Minoda was the most persistent and vehement.[8] He followed up with a longer article that focused on Tanaka's argument that Shinto should be included as a religion regulated under the law. Like Ono, he zeroed in on Tanaka's thinking as a form of dualism, which he called "medieval" and "an unpatriotic ideology" (*han-kokuminshugi shisō*) (Minoda 1928, pp. 517–548). While he added little that was new to his original critique of the book, he amplified his points and developed major sections attacking Christianity that revealed how central his hatred of Christianity was to his interpretation of Tanaka and to his own politics. Tanaka did not bother replying to Minoda this time.

In spite of the negative stance Tanaka had taken on the compatibility of the Catholic faith and shrine visits, the Ministry of Education included his book *Law, Religion and Social Life* in its 1933 publication of officially recommended books.[9] There are several possible reasons for this favorable view of Tanaka's work that was written as a criticism of the government's position that Shinto was a civic duty and not a religion. Admiral Saitō Makoto had been appointed prime minister in the wake of the May 15, 1932 terrorist incident by radical Imperial Navy officers who assassinated Prime Minister Inukai Tsuyoshi. Emperor Hirohito had expressed his desire for "a man of good character, while absolutely rejecting someone with Fascist leanings" (National Diet Library, "Modern Japan in Archives"). Prime Minister Saitō put together a national unity cabinet, and part of that unity was a globalist attitude that welcomed the Christian minority. As part of the gesture toward a national unity cabinet, he kept his predecessor's Minister of Education Hatoyama Ichirō, a graduate of the Imperial University of Tokyo Law Faculty and a Christian. Hatoyama had several reasons to view Tanaka's work in a favorable light, and the progress made between his Ministry and the Catholic Church towards an understanding on shrine visits was certainly one. But after ten years of being viciously attacked as a traitor (*hi-kokumin*) by right-wing nationalists like Minoda for his globalism, Tanaka found that the Ministry of Education quietly had dropped his work from their later list of recommended books (Tanaka 1961, p. 60). By 1943 when the war was raging, the political climate had certainly changed enough that Tanaka's argument for moral limits on the state, based on global principles, no longer was warmly received.

Notes

1. See Tanaka (1924, pp. 24–25), and his citation there to Theodor Sternberg, *Entwickelungslinie der Rechtsphilosophie*.
2. Hanzawa centers his discussion of *Hō to shūkyō to shakai seikatsu* on Tanaka's idea of Man's dual nature (*ningen no nigensei*), but he attributes this idea to Fr. Iwashita and holds that Tanaka took it in his own particular (Lutheran?) fashion that was difficult to reconcile with the Natural Law (Hanzawa 1993, pp. 145, 178). I think the evidence is stronger that Tanaka got the idea of "Man's dual nature" from his reading of Solovyov in the early 1920s before he had met Fr. Iwashita. See Chapter 1. Moreover, Hanzawa's understanding of the concept of *nigensei*

as "polarity" (*poraritēi*) (Hanzawa 1993, p. 178) contrasts with Tanaka's own gloss of the concept as "dualism" (*dearizumu*) in Tanaka (1922, p. 12). Araki follows Tanaka's gloss of the concept as "dualism" and places his development of the concept in *Hō to shūkyō to shakai seikatsu* in the context of Tanaka's 1922 lecture, while showing how a very Catholic emphasis on the role of works emerges in the 1927 book. Araki (2012, pp. 108, 114).

3. This line is often misrepresented, as it is on the Wikipedia stub, as denouncing "the proposition that the state should be separated from the Church as a thesis absolutely false, a most pernicious error." The distinction between "must be" and "should be" is an important one, and germane to Tanaka's discussion on religious freedom.
4. This appears to be the earliest instance of the maxim *ubi societas ibi ius* that would appear frequently thereafter in Tanaka's writings.
5. Here Tanaka seems to be following the vocabulary of Stammler who distinguished between concepts or categories (*Begriff*) and the ideal (*Idee*) of law, in which the latter "represents the goal of a completely systematic explanation in terms of means and end" which never is achieved. See Sabine (1933, p. 335).
6. Minoda had not only just attacked the Protestant Nambara Shigeru in the same journal (*Genri Nihon*, December 1925), but he also had written a long rebuttal of fellow anti-communist Tsuchida Kyōson's proposal for Japan to open diplomatic relations with the Holy See (*Genri Nihon*, April 1923). Minoda's obsessive attack on Christianity also is apparent in the content of his criticism of Tanaka below.
7. Ono Seiichirō (1891–1986) was a specialist in criminal law who also was deeply involved in Buddhist research, especially on Shinran. He was purged from public office from 1946 to 1951 for his position during the war supporting the attack on Takigawa Yukitoki for being a liberal (the Takigawa Incident of 1933). Ono's position in that dispute, already prefigured in his critique of Tanaka Kōtarō above, was in defense of the state against Takigawa's "normative illegality" which Ono saw as a violation of the state's legal order. Christianity was centrally involved in the Takigawa Incident, as it was Takigawa's lecture at Chuo University on Tolstoy's "Resurrection" that sparked denunciations of him as a liberal.
8. On Minoda's attack on globalist legal scholars of his day, by all means see Jason Morgan's recent excellent article, "Catholic Critiques of Statism in Interwar Japan: Minoda Muneki, Suehiro Izutarō, and Tanaka Kōtarō."
9. Tanaka's *Hō to shūkyō to shakai seikatsu* was placed on the longer list of 45 "books introduced" rather than the shorter list of 7 "recommended books." It still was ranked higher than 34 volumes that were merely listed as "selected." See Monbushō, ed. (1933, pp. 3, 61–66).

References

Araki Shin'ichirō. 2012. Tanaka Kōtarō no kyōiku mokutekikan seiritsu ni ataeta Jakku Maritan no eikyō. In Nagasaki Junshin Daigaku Katorikku Shakai Fukushi Kenkyūjo, ed., *Katorikku shakai fukushi kenkyū*, vol. 12, pp. 93–151.

Hanzawa, Takamaro. 1993. *Kindai nihon no katorishizumu: shisōshi-teki kōsatsu*. Tokyo: Misuzu Shobō.

Inoue, Shigeru. 1974. Hōri tankyū no tetsugaku: shoki ni kakuritsu sareta kihon shisei. *Hōtetsugaku nenpō* 1973: 145–167.

Kasuya, Tomosuke. 1999. Ningen no nigensei–Tanaka Kōtarō no manifesuto. *Jurisuto* 1155 (May): 59–61.

Kotani, Yumi. 2011. Tanaka Kōtarō ni okeru shizen hō shisō to jinkaku gainen. *Katorikku Kyōiku Kenkyū* 28: 16–29.

M.K. 1927. Ronri yori omoki gutai-teki seikatsu yōkyū: Tanaka Kōtarō cho *Hō to shūkyō to shakai seikatsu* o yonde. *Teikoku daigaku shimbun*, number 206 (April 25), p. 3.

Minoda, Muneki. 1927. Tanaka Kōtarō-shi no *Hō to shūkyō to shakai seikatsu* o hyō su. *Genri nihon* (March): 26–28.

———. 1928. Tanaka Kōtarō hakase no *Hō to shūkyō to shakai seikatsu* o hyō shite jinja tai shūkyō mondai o keppan su. *Genri Nihon* (July): 517–548; reprinted in Takeuchi Yō, ed., *Minoda Muneki zenshū*. Tokyo: Kashiwa Shobō, 2004, vol. 3, pp. 571–602.

Monbushō, ed. 1933. *Shisō mondai ni kan suru ryōsho senshō*. Tokyo: Monbusho Gakuseibu.

Morgan, Jason. 2018. Catholic Critiques of Statism in Interwar Japan: Minoda Muneki, Suehiro Izutarō, and Tanaka Kōtarō. *Logos* 21 (3): 35–66.

National Diet Library, ed. Modern Japan in Archives, Crisis in Constitutional Politics. http://www.ndl.go.jp/modern/e/cha4/description02.html. Accessed 10 July 2015.

Ono, Seiichirō. 1927. Tanaka Kōtarō no kincho o hyō su. *Hōritsu shunjū* (June): 71–75.

Pius X. 1906. *Vehementer Nos*. http://w2.vatican.va/content/pius-x/en/encyclicals/documents/hf_p-x_enc_11021906_vehementer-nos.html. Accessed 18 June 2015.

Sabine, George H. 1933. Rudolf Stammler's Critical Philosophy of Law. *Cornell Law Review* 18 (3): pp. 321–350.

Tanaka, Kōtarō. 1922. Rippō no jōshū. *Seisho no kenkyū* (December): 11–16.

———. 1923. Shōhō no kihon kannen o sadamuru hitsuyō ni tsuite. *Hōgaku Shimbun* 33 (10); reprinted in *Tanaka Kōtarō chosakushū* (hereafter, *TKc*). Tokyo: Shunjū Sha, 1954, vol. 7, pp. 1–7.

———. 1924. Shōhōgaku no ninmu. *Hōgaku kyōkai zasshi* 42 (3–5); reprinted in *TKc* vol. 7, pp. 9–63.

———. 1927a. *Hō to shūkyō to shakai seikatsu*. Tokyo: Kaizō Sha.
———. 1927b. Hō to shūkyō to shakai seikatsu no ni san no hihyō ni kotau (ge). *Teikoku daigaku shimbun*, number 212 (June 6), p. 3.
———. 1961. *Watakushi no rirekisho*. Tokyo: Shunjū Sha.

CHAPTER 3

Tanaka's Theory of World Law

Abstract This central chapter outlines Tanaka's theory of global law as presented in his prize-winning, three volume study *A Theory of World Law* (1932–1934). Inspired by Ernst Zitelmann's short essay that suggested the possibility of World Law, Tanaka developed the idea at great length. His key argument was that law comes from society, not the State or the nation (*Volk*), and that the emergence of a world society implied the existence of World Law. This idea of globalism as the essence of law laid the foundation for his critiques of Nazism and Fascism, and for his defense against Marxists like Tosaka Jun. The chapter shows the troubles Tanaka faced as Dean of the Law Faculty of the Imperial University of Tokyo in the late 1930s and into the wartime as nationalists and militarists attacked globalists like Tanaka. It concludes with Tanaka's contribution to futile efforts to expedite an end to the war during 1943–1945.

Keywords World law · Nation vs. State · Ernst Zitelmann
ubi societas ibi ius · Alfred E. Zimmern · Sannenkai group

K. M. Doak, *Tanaka Kōtarō and World Law*, Global Political Thinkers,
https://doi.org/10.1007/978-3-030-02035-4_3

> We need an authority in the spiritual life that can guarantee the objectivity of what we believe in. Also, we need a Church that is sufficiently organized and is under the control of an authority that resists individualization or socialization, that is the individual evils and social evils. That Church is the *Gemeinschaft* of all humanity as it exists in spiritual life; it must be based on a trans-ethnic, trans-State, trans-class principle of organization that includes all the world's people. There is already one such religion. It is the Catholic Church. (Tanaka 1930, pp. 605–606)

As we saw above in Chapter 2, Tanaka had begun conceiving the project of World Law as early as 1924 and incorporated outlines of his idea on World Law in his first publication, the 1927 *Law, Religion and Social Life*. That work was written in response to the problem of religious freedom, both as a global and domestic issue. But Tanaka realized that to get the relationship of religion and the State right, a better understanding of law and justice was necessary. This deeper problem was the substance of his multivolume study, *A Theory of World Law* which he submitted as his dissertation in 1929 and for which he received the degree of Doctor of Law in April of that year. After many revisions and additions, Iwanami Shoten published it in three volumes that came out individually in 1932, 1933, and 1934. Tanaka dedicated the work to Professor Yamada Saburōand Nitobe Inazō, "two leaders of the international spirit in Japan" (Tanaka 1932b, p. 15). But internationalism was quickly waning in Japan by the time the last volume appeared, and Tanaka's argument in favor of World Law was increasingly seen as unpatriotic by those in the rising nationalist movement. In his introduction to the 1948 republication of *A Theory of World Law*, Tanaka captured succinctly how the work was received when it was first published:

> Volume one was published in 1932, which is to say the year after the Manchurian Incident. It upset those in the statist-ethnic nationalist camp (*kokkashugi-teki minzokushugi-teki jin'ei*) whowere then just rising to prominence, and it became the target of their attacks. When it received the Asahi Prize in spring of 1935, these attacks intensified and even reached the Asahi Newspaper Company, and those scholars in the Imperial Academy who had indicated their support for my work also got in trouble for having done so. (Tanaka 1948, p. 3)

Tanaka's combination of "statism" and "ethnic nationalism" in one phrase may seem idiosyncratic, but it goes right to the heart of his globalism that, in contrast to more common forms of globalism, sought to retain a legitimate role for ethnic nationalism, separated from the State, as a valid force for democracy. In his jurisprudence, ethnic nationalism was mostly a danger when it was linked to the State or when either the ethnic nation or the State were taken as the ultimate limitation on law and justice (Fig. 3.1).

Based on the maxim *ubi societas ibi ius* (wherever there is society, there is law), and on his argument that States and nations are not the only forms of society, Tanaka argued that every kind of society had a role to play in the realization of justice at multiple levels—a position that would become more popular in later years in the theory of subsidiarity. For Tanaka, society was not merely a sub-State mode of organization, but also included global society that reached over and beyond the State. He insisted in his introduction that "my position is not that of individualistic cosmopolitanism. It is merely one that, while recognizing that the State and the ethnic nation have their own cultural and moral missions,

Fig. 3.1 Tanaka Kōtarō, ca. 1935 (with permission from Misuzu Shobō, Ltd., Tokyo)

seeks a way that the State and the ethnic nation can reach their true maturation. And it believes this must be done through a reconciliation of statism, internationalism, ethnic nationalism, and global humanism" (Tanaka 1932b, p. 11). A good deal of what makes Tanaka's *Theory of World Law* original was in fact this systematic effort to develop a jurisprudence that might reconcile universalism and particularism, nationalism and internationalism, the State and the ethnic nation—indeed the very tensions that were tearing apart not only Japan but the world during the early 1930s. His was a bold experiment.

Tanaka laid out his basic argument in the first chapter of *A Theory of World Law*. He openly acknowledged his inspiration from a 1919 reprint of Ernst Zitelmann's brief 1889 essay, "Die Möglichkeit eines Weltrechts" (The Possibility of a World Law). Although Zitelmann's essay was largely ignored in his time, it attracted scholarly attention after 1906 when Eugen Ehrlich enthusiastically introduced Zitelmann's book on private international law—and indeed, it has enjoyed a modest reception even more recently in English literature on international law.[1] Tanaka noted a tendency among legal scholars to ridicule the idea of World Law, either because it seemed to reject State sovereignty and positive law or because it was incompatible with the idea that all social phenomena should be judged from the position of ethnic nationalism. But Tanaka maintained that his *Theory of World Law* could withstand such criticism because first, World Law was not incompatible with State sovereignty nor did it reject the significance of ethnic nationality. World Law simply "does not claim that State sovereignty is absolute, nor does it exaggerate the value of ethnic nationality for the law" (Tanaka 1932b, p. 7). And in both arguments, World Law was consistent with trends in legal scholarship at the time that placed certain limits on State sovereignty while also moving away from the Historical School's extreme position that the ethnic nation was the source of law.

Tanaka's approach to World Law was novel and challenging. As he put it, "research on World Law takes comparative legal studies as its tool and thus in its empirical method will not fall into the rationalism of the Enlightenment Natural Law nor in its effort to expand its limits of inquiry will it fall into the errors of the Historical School, nor … will it fall into the superficiality of historicism or the comparative legal scholars who consistently fail to consider the very nature of law" (Tanaka 1932b, p. 14). World Law was not an excuse for ignoring positive laws and the particularities of social reality. Rather, it was "a bridge between positive law and jurisprudence" that sought to fill the gap in legal studies that remained between "law and morality, law and customs, law and religion, law and economics, *et cetera*" (Tanaka 1932b, p. 16). Moreover, Tanaka addressed the general skepticism toward theory by reminding his readers that while scholarship grows out of attention to particular phenomena, without a theory to give direction and meaning to the results of particular findings, a scholar cannot produce original work and is left with blind results, "unable to contribute to the progress of legal principles in general" (Tanaka 1932b, p. 12).

Tanaka did not have to create his theory of World Law out of whole cloth, nor was he interested merely in a new abstract theory that was not grounded in legal and social reality. The first order of business was to clarify the meaning of law as a concept and, at the same time, to clarify the concept of society as a reality distinct from the State. Tanaka astutely rejected both a-theoretical empiricism in the social sciences as "falling into the vice of positivism" and the neo-Kantian penchant for pure methodology (*Methodenreinheit*) as "falling into mere subjectivism that had no grounding in real life" (Tanaka 1932b, p. 30). Tanaka's pragmatic approach to World Law sought to identify those spheres where World Law had applicability and those where it did not. In discovering those spheres, he found support in Ferdinand Tönnies's sociology that identified distinctive social types of *Gemeinschaft* and *Gesellschaft*, emotional particular communities and rational universal communities (Tanaka 1932b, p. 24). The impulse of the former type of society mandated particular communities like States and ethnic nations, but the reality of the latter universal type of community revealed the limitations, particularly for law and justice, of the former. What Tanaka sought in his theory of World Law was not a de-legitimation of local communities in the name of an idealistic globalism, but rather a realistic accounting of how we are all both particular and universal, local and global, at the same time. What he found lacking was a legal theory that could fully account for this rich dimension of social life.

Before outlining his pragmatic approach to World Law, Tanaka critically explored what he called our need to "be liberated from the two preconceptions that consciously or subconsciously bind" us: the linking of law to the State (*kokka*) and the linking of law to ethnic nationality (*minzoku*) (Tanaka 1932b, p. 42). He cited Georg Jellinek's view of law as "the means by which we secure the living conditions of society" (*Sicherung der Lebensbedingungen der Gesellschaft*) and Rudolph Stammler's recognition of "law as a condition of social legality" (*das Recht als Bedingung sozialer Gesetzmässigkeit*) to emphasize that even positivist and idealist jurists had both recognized the necessity of law for society. He then suggested that the old maxim *ubi societas ibi ius* can also be reversed: *ubi ius ibi societas* (wherever there is law, there is society) (Tanaka 1932b, pp. 46–47). Tanaka emphasized the sociological dimensions of law, rejecting the positivism of John Austin and others who reduced law to the command of the sovereign and defining the essence of law instead as related to the common good (*bonum commune*) of society. This meant that law was essentially about more than political control; it was essentially about the problem of justice, a point that Tanaka noted was made more explicit in the linguistic connections to justice in the terms for law in many languages other than English (*ius, Recht, droit, diritto, derecho, pravo*) (Tanaka 1932b, p. 60). Nonetheless, Tanaka accepted the fact that law is not mere moral suasion but does indeed possess a coercive element. This coercion, however, was neither the essential element in law nor did it do any violence to human dignity because the purpose of law is to elevate Man to his full potential. Whether it be moral issues like theft, murder or adultery, or technical areas like negotiable instruments, Tanaka argued that the law took Man as he was (neither angel nor beast) and set down rules that enabled him to realize those needs and secure the rights that legitimately belonged to him. In short, the nature of law was not to impose an arbitrary and external will on others, but to answer social needs that are endemic to Man's nature as a social animal. The idea that law was inherently linked to the State was the result of a nineteenth century trend, an aberration in the general trend in the history of law over the centuries where law was consistently understood as essentially linked to the question of justice. And, Tanaka concluded, during the early twentieth century, legal scholars from a variety of perspectives (sociological, Historical School, Natural Law) have raised serious critiques of the theory that law emanates from the will of the State or the command of the sovereign.

Tanaka's own conclusion to his chapter on "The Concept of Law and the Concept of the State" is important and concise enough to quote here:

> To summarize: the concept of law does not take as its main element State sovereignty or the powers of coercion that emanate from it. The basis of law must be sought in justice, and only then does law acquire its own particular value that is distinct from actual power. Law in this sense is required by the sum total of the communal life of Man, and this is not something necessarily limited to life in a State. The existence of law in this sense must be sought directly in society itself. Since society exists both above the State and below the State, there are multifarious laws in accordance with

> the many different types of societies. This is why one cannot recognize as law only Statist laws. To recover law through a sense of justice as directly found in social life itself—in contrast to law as a monopoly of the State—has been the goal of the arguments in this chapter. In doing so, we have opened one *via negativa* to the initial recognition of World Law. (Tanaka 1932b, pp. 151–152)

Tanaka believed that by showing the existence of law in society and pointing out that some forms of society were global ("above the State"), he had cleared away at least half of the major obstacles for his eventual positive argument for World Law. This is what he meant by having opened a "*via negativa*" to World Law. There remained one other obstacle to a truly global understanding of law and that was one that came from outside the statist approach to law, one that he himself had drawn on in building his challenge to the State from the position of society.

That other obstacle to a global law or World Law was the belief that law was an expression of a particular *minzoku* (nation, defined ethnically). This position, which Tanaka associated with the nineteenth century German Historical School, drew much from the sociological approach that had pried the concept of law away from the State-centered sovereignty theory of law. But it made a major mistake in reducing law to the expression of the will of a particular *minzoku*. Tanaka did not deny all aspects of the relativity of law in application, but the Historical School had taken this relativity to the extreme of defining the nature of law itself. Tanaka realized that the first order of business was to define what exactly a *minzoku* was, if it were to be the source and limitation of law. He surveyed the leading theorists on national identity of his time (especially Ernest Barker, George Peabody Gooch, Bernard Joseph, Ramsay Muir, William B. Pillsbury, Ernst Renan, and Alfred Zimmern).[2] He accepted their conclusion that the nation (*minzoku*) was ultimately a subjective mode of group consciousness without any final, objective definition (Tanaka 1932b, pp. 211–214). This subjective nature of the nation did not disqualify it from social relevance. But it did make it impossible to serve as the foundation for law.

Tanaka's position on the nation was largely identical with that of Zimmern's ideas as expressed in an article on which Tanaka drew heavily. Zimmern held that the nation was a legitimate form of group identity and that in their day "the real trouble in fact is not nationalism … . The indictment should be drawn not against nations but against states; not against statesmen acting as the spokesmen of nationalities and the interpreters of nationalism but against statesmen acting as the instruments of sovereign states … [and their] selfish policies" (Zimmern 1923, p. 116; Cf. Tanaka 1932b, pp. 194–195). The significance of Zimmern's understanding of nation and State is elucidated by Barker who wrote that Zimmern was merely developing an idea expressed decades earlier by Lord Acton: that the nation and the State were not necessarily identical. Barker did not wholly subscribe to the view of Lord Actonand Zimmern, but he did an admirable job of describing it. As he wrote, for them:

> Nationality … is a social fact … . It belongs to the independent life of the mind, which goes its way in the spaces which lie outside the scheme of politics … . The State, on the other hand, is an impartial and impersonal structure: it is a scheme of organization: it is a political and legal fact. The nation and the State belong to separate departments. The nation, as a social fact or form of existence, may content itself with the social expression of its peculiar attributes. The State, as a political scheme, may safely embrace a variety of national cultures, if only it is wise enough to practice the virtue of toleration. (Barker 1927, pp. 251–252)[3]

It is not surprising that Tanaka would embrace the Actonian position on the multinational State when we recall that he shared with Lord Acton the experience of being a minority Catholic in a dominant non-Catholic country, and that both England and Japan had histories of ruthless persecution of their Catholic minorities. This shared history gave both Lord Acton and Tanaka a respect for groups founded on religious identities but also a pragmatic understanding that modern political organizations like the State could not and should not be limited to majority ethnic and/or religious groups.

As a jurist, Tanaka approached this question of the role of ethnic (and religious) groups in terms of the relationship of law and ethnic nationality (*minzoku*). He did not deny that there was a relationship between law and the ethnic nation, but he argued that many scholars, particularly those influenced by the German Historical School, were getting that relationship exactly backward. They argued that law was a product of the ethnic nation rather than recognizing that social groups like ethnic nations were being influenced by global conceptions of the law. Even Barker, who had tried to negate the German Historical School, had gone too far in the other direction in arguing that, while the law was not the product of a nation, still the law could create particular national sentiments (for example, the English nation). For Tanaka, the key point was that while "law may be thought of as the most powerful influence in shaping national unity" because "law is the framework for social life and promotes unity in State life and in other actual social lives, it is nonetheless wholly inappropriate for creating spiritual forms of existence like the nation (*minzoku*) " (Tanaka 1932b, p. 260, n. 1). Note that Tanaka saw the role of spiritual issues like religion in the formation of ethnic nations. He did not reduce nationality to religious identity, and he rejected the idea that natural elements like geography or race were determinant of nation. Drawing on leading liberal theorists who had concluded that the nation was largely a form of consciousness, he saw religion as one of those modes of consciousness that formed social groups, even ethnic nationality. The overarching consideration was how to reconcile such groups with others within the political structures of the State, and by extension how to reconcile different States with each other in a broader concept of the world. In both case, the solution rested on a concept of law that was not produced by and for a single nation or ethnic group.

Articulating this concept of the law, one that was neither an effect of the State nor of the ethnic nation, was the main task of Tanaka's *Theory of World Law*. As befitting a specialist in commercial law, Tanaka found the basis of World Law in economic relations of exchange that often eluded full recognition in either municipal law or international law as practiced in his day. The classic understanding of international law was premised on an economic theory that divided the world economy into national economies (*kokumin keizai*). In response to this limitation, economists like Bernard Harms had outlined a new economic theory for the new international law of Hugo Krabbe, Léon Duguit and Hans Kelsen by recognizing only "particular economies" (*Einzelwirtschaften*) rather than national economies. In Tanaka's view, the inter-relationship of particular economies and national economies gave rise to a new, distinctive economic unit, the world economy. This world economy is in turn comprised of both the international economy and what he called "the world people's economy" (*banmin keizai*), both of which would fall under the jurisdiction of World Law.[4] World Law then is divided into laws covering the international economy and laws covering the world people's economy. The world people's economy is regulated by international civil law or unified law, which Tanaka notes may also be described as World Law in the narrow sense, whereas the international economy is regulated by international law. Laws governing the world people's economy belong to the civil law branch of World Law; laws governing the international economy belong to the public law branch of World Law. Tanaka admitted that this schema of World Law was not perfect, as already Harms had pointed out the ways municipal laws often have international implications (for example, immigration laws, labor laws, export organization laws, and the like), and thus national economic demands sometimes must yield to internationalist ideals in the interests of healthy world economic growth. But in the end, Tanaka concluded that the problems raised by Harms could be resolved simply by achieving a better reconciliation between national economies and the world economy through international economic conferences that could address such problems through the traditional mechanisms of international law (treaties) (Tanaka 1934a, pp. 716–718). In short, the remaining problems were merely a matter of adjusting the codification of World Law into statutory laws through a better understanding of the fluid social and economic realities of the day.

These fluid global economic realities suggested to Tanaka the limits of State sovereignty as a sufficient foundation for justice and international law. But the matter of justice was not limited to economic tensions; recent developments in international law, he noted, had much to do with the work of the League of Nations and its various committees that had contributed greatly to the establishment of a true, international society (*kokusai shakai*). By the 1930s, international law was no longer focused merely on resolving economic and political tensions among States; it had evolved to organizing modes of cooperation on matters as diverse as administrative, economic, technological, and even moral issues. With the evident development of international society, Tanaka believed—in keeping with his favorite legal maxim, *ubi societas ibi ius*—that "international law had become the public law of world society, namely World Public Law" [*sekai kōhō*] (Tanaka 1934a, pp. 722–723).[5] Thus, it was important to bring more clarity to the forms of justice that would underwrite World Law. Tanaka found a hint in the fact that, as traditional international law had attempted to regulate relations of contestation and cooperation between States, it had nonetheless remained under the influence of a theory of justice that was traceable to Aquinas and through him, back to Aristotle: conflicts between States were governed by the concept of commutative justice (*iustitia commutative*), the form of justice that in municipal law was found in civil law. With World Law, however, the relations among individuals have to be adjudicated in the absence of a World State and thus should be considered as relations subject to public law and under the concepts of distributive justice (*iustitia distributive*) or legal or general justice (*iustitia legalis od. generalis*). Distributive justice imposes obligations on international organizations in their relations with member States; legal or general justice imposes obligations on member States in their relations with international organizations. In short, Tanaka pointed out that the ultimate foundation of international law as World Law is the same as that of municipal law: both stem from the Natural Law. And, he concluded, only through the Natural Law can we begin to envision the unification of municipal law and World Law (Tanaka 1934a, pp. 723–724).

Tanaka's *Theory of World Law* was warmly received, winning the Asahi Prize in 1935 after the third volume was published. As Seiichi Anan noted, "In 1934 he successfully completed his great work, *World Law*, which was highly thought of by all jurists, even his opponents. This was an epoch-making work, a history of natural law which went far beyond the mere importing or digesting of theories which had originated in foreign countries" (Anan 1962, p. 112). Yet, he had his critics. The year 1935 was a crucial watershed in Japanese political culture, with Marxists and conservative nationalists at each other's throats. Tanaka was caught in the middle. The leading Marxist intellectual Tosaka Jun found Tanaka's views too conservative and was particularly incensed by his Catholicism. He wrote an open letter to Tanaka in the *Yomiuri* newspaper in 1935, challenging him to defend himself against the charge that his Catholic views were not in fact globalist but, in their rejection of moral libertarianism, were essentially on the side of right-wing nationalists (Tosaka 1935, p. 10). It was an unfair charge, as Tanaka had been one of the earliest public critics of Nazi ideology, publishing criticisms of Mussolini's and Hitler's movements as early as 1932 in leading newspapers and magazines.[6] Tanaka replied to Tosaka, explaining patiently how his Catholicism "does not lend its support to the violent view of the State. It is vigilant and critical when the State ignores the Natural Law, that is, morality that has become a healthy common sense" (Tanaka 1935, p. 10). No doubt, Tanaka did not convince Tosaka or other Marxists that Catholicism was on their side; but he did make a powerful case that his views were every bit as global as theirs and not an ally of the narrow nationalists and the extreme rightwing.

Tanaka had even more trouble from his critics on the political right. His old nemesis Minoda Muneki came back in force to condemn Tanaka's latest book. Minoda's attack on Tanaka incorporated a sub-attack on the well-known liberal scholar Minobe Tatsukichi for praising Tanaka's effort to establish World Law on a concept of world society (Minoda 1938, pp. 109–117). Historians have generally focused on Minoda's attack on Minobe and his "organ theory" of the emperor, without mention of his attack on Tanaka (for example, Mitchell 1976, pp. 151–155). Certainly, as a member of the House of Peers, Minobe had more public stature than his university law colleague, the younger Tanaka. But Tanaka and Minobe shared much in their legal theories, and Tanaka's global law theory was indebted to Minobe's work. As we saw above in Chapter 2, Minoda had been a vehement and public critic of Tanaka from the beginning of Tanaka's publishing career, writing a short article condemning *Law, Religion and Social Life* in the March 1928 issue of his journal *Genri Nihon* and, following Tanaka's response, a much longer article in the July issue of the same journal. Now, after Tanaka's prize-winning three volume *A Theory of World Law* was published, Minoda turned up the heat, redoubling his attacks and repeating his claim that Tanaka's views were unacceptable because they stemmed from his Catholic faith which was "unscientific and anti-*kokutai*" (Minoda 1938, p. 27). The argument about the *kokutai* (national polity) was of course the same one leveled against Minobe (and many others) and came in the midst of a concerted effort to reject globalism in favor of a concept of Japanese national identity based on the redefinition of the national polity in the 1937 government publication of *The True Meaning of the Kokutai*.[7] As Jason Morgan has pointed out recently in an excellent article on Tanaka and Minoda, "what especially riled Minoda was Tanaka's Catholicism, and in particular Tanaka's advocacy of a globalist instantiation of the Natural Law that Tanaka called 'world law'" (Morgan et al. 2018, p. 51).

In the midst of raging nationalism and a simultaneous withdrawal to regionalism if not outright isolationism during the late 1930s, Tanaka found ways to remain an active globalist intellectual. In December 1935 the Center for International Cultural Relations sent Tanaka to Italy for nearly a year as an exchange professor. He traveled to the United States and across Europe, lecturing at various universities on his theory of World Law, global culture and Catholicism. In contrast to his first trip to Europe, some fifteen years earlier, politics—especially rising fascism—was an unavoidable topic. Tanaka attended a preliminary Conference of the Intellectual Cooperation Committee of the League of Nations in Madrid as an observer, and he certainly was at home among these leading cosmopolitan intellectuals who were desperately seeking a means of avoiding the impending war. He was much less comfortable meeting Mussolini. But the experience in fascist Italy was a transformative one. Tanaka himself called it "a turning point in my life" (Tanaka 1961, p. 62) and Hanzawa Takamaro saw the experience as a determinant one, taking Tanaka from his youthful aestheticism to maturity as a "public man" (Hanzawa 1993, pp. 216–218, cited in Shibasaki 2015, p. 52). Tanaka certainly did not withdraw from the challenges of public life. He continued to publish, including an essay on his experiences in Italy in the leading cultural magazine *Bungei Shunjū*, and in June of 1937 he collected many of his earlier essays that had been published between 1923 and 1936 and republished them in an important volume called *The Basis of Education* (*kyōyō*) *and Culture*. Among those essays was his 1934 article "An Intellectual Historical Analysis and Critique of the Nazi Concept of Law." The most recent among them was his 1936 article "The Idea of an International Cultural Movement." In his introduction, Tanaka criticized both *jiyūshugi* (liberalism/libertarianism) and cultural imperialism, saying that his interest in culture was only in the value it holds "for perfecting Man's moral mission" (Tanaka 1937, "Jo," p. 3). And he left no doubt that the best understanding of culture for that task was located in tradition of philosophical Scholasticism.

Tanaka's globalism was put to the test soon after his return to Japan. In April 1937 he was appointed Dean of the Law Faculty at the Imperial University of Tokyo by President Hiraga Yuzuru. Now, in a highly visible position, Tanaka came under increasing pressure from all sides. Minoda's attack on Tanaka, even dredging up his earlier work, was not without effect. Baron Mimurodo Yukimitsu, who a few years earlier had attacked Minobe Tatsukichi for his organ theory, on February 1, 1938 attacked Tanaka in the House of Peers for having written in his *Law, Religion and Social Life* that "it is not possible to make the entire nation worship the ancient Shinto gods" and "the best policy would be to abolish the custom of having elementary schools make nationalistic [*kokutai-teki*] visits to Shinto shrines" (*Yomiuri Shimbun* 1938, p. 2). Addressing Kido Kōichi, the Minister of Education, Baron Mimurodo exclaimed, "You've got a professor as Dean of the Law Faculty of the Imperial University who knows nothing of the spirit of the *kokutai*!" (Mimurodo, cited in Tachibana 2005, p. 398). Minister Kido and General Suetsugu Nobumasa, the Home Minister, both promised to look into the matter and take appropriate measures. Eventually, Tanaka was summoned to the Imperial Diet to answer the questions raised by Baron Mimurodo. Before leaving for the Diet, Tanaka told his Catholic friends who were worried about him that "I wrote in a book that if you consider shrines and temples as religious, then it is not a good idea to compel student groups to visit such places. However, now the State does not consider the Yasukuni Shrine to be a religious institution, so there shouldn't be any problem." Tanaka was referring to assurances the Ministry of Education had made officially to the Catholic Church in 1932 (five years after his book had been published) that visits to Yasukuni Shrine were not of a religious nature. This argument not only reassured Tanaka's Catholic friends, but it also left Baron Mimurodo with nothing to say after Tanaka testified on the basis of these facts in the Diet (Takamine 1974, p. 460). Much to Mimurodo's dismay, Tanaka was not removed from his position either as Dean or as an imperial university professor.

Looking back in recent years, Tachibana Takashi is quite right to situate this controversy within the broader tensions between "World Law" and "Clarification of the *Kokutai*" as the key debate in Japanese public discourse during those years. Ultimately, it boiled down to a battle between those who "thought that each ethnic nation had its own source of law in its own ethnic gods" and those who thought "they needed to make a universal human society by discovering a universal foundation for law somewhere other than in an ethnic god" (Tachibana 2005, p. 406). This broader ideological conflict between nationalists and globalists set the stage for what later became known as the "Hiraga Purge" of professors in the Economics Department of the Imperial University of Tokyo, a purge in which Tanaka played a decisive role. The reasons that led to the purge are complex and beyond the scope of this book; suffice it to say that the Department of Economics had long suffered from dysfunctional strife between two main camps: the leftists centered on Kawai Eijirō and the rightists centered on Hijikata Seibi. Kawai had made some indiscrete comments against the military that led to tremendous pressure on Hiraga's predecessor to fire him. When Hiraga assumed the presidency, it was clear he was expected to do something about Kawai. Tanaka was quite sympathetic to Kawai, and in fact after a right-wing student Odamura Torajirō verbally attacked Kawai (and Yokota Kisaburō) in September 1938, Tanaka disciplined the student who was ultimately suspended from the university (Urabe 2004, p. 68). It was Tanaka who came up with the idea that, if Kawai (who loosely belonged to the globalist camp) had to go, then the rightists had to sacrifice their leader

Hijikata who was essentially Minoda Muneki's spy among the university faculty (Takeuchi 2001, pp. 212–213). President Hiraga took Tanaka's advice and fired both Hijikata and Kawai on January 28, 1939. Thirteen economics professors resigned in protest. The move had broken the impasse in the economics department, but it also reduced the department to a shadow of its former self.

An unintended consequence of Tanaka's effort to preserve university autonomy was that many in his own department turned against him. The Law Faculty had members close to Hijikata's faction. But what hurt Tanaka most was that some of his old friends, especially Protestants like Nambara Shigeru and Yanaihara Tadao, joined in condemning him for what they felt was a violation of academic freedom. They were not open to Tanaka's argument that he had worked in the larger interest of protecting university autonomy from militarist pressures and that they were only interested in their own personal privileges. Indeed, they seemed to have quickly forgotten Tanaka's leadership in resisting General Araki Sadao's efforts as Education Minister just months earlier to deprive the university faculty of its autonomy (Marshall 1978, pp. 546–547). The Law Faculty squabbles were reported in the major newspapers, with growing calls for Tanaka to resign. Ultimately, he was forced to resign after lasting through six contentious faculty meetings. As he later reflected, it was the first time in history a dean of the Law Faculty had to resign for reasons other than illness (Tanaka 1961, p. 70).

Tanaka's resignation as dean also created new possibilities for expressing his globalism at a critical time in Japanese history. Freed from administrative responsibility, Tanaka was able to accept an invitation from the American Division of the Foreign Ministry to travel to six countries in Latin America from May to October 1939 as an informal diplomat. Tanaka's appointment was not unrelated to his globalism and his Catholic faith. He followed in the footsteps of another Japanese Catholic, Rear Admiral Yamamoto Shinji (Stefano) who had gone on an informal diplomatic mission to Latin America, as well as to North America and Europe the previous year. On his mission, Tanaka engaged with leading intellectuals and politicians in Brazil, Argentina, Chile, Peru, Panama and Mexico, even having personal audiences with President Getúlio Vargas of Brazil and President Roberto María Ortiz of Argentina.[8] Drawing on that experience, Tanaka published many articles and books on Latin America, often emphasizing the globalism of the Catholic faith as a means of connecting peoples of different cultures around the world.

Soon after Tanaka's return to Japan in late 1939, the tensions between globalism and the rising nationalist militarism grew intense. Even so, as late as May 1941, Tanaka's globalism did not prevent him from being named a member of the Imperial Academy. But by December 1941, Tanaka's position was becoming increasingly precarious. He was proposed for another informal diplomatic mission, this time to French Indochina. But one week before his departure, he was told by Bureau Chief Hirose of the Intelligence Agency to cancel the trip since they had information the Japanese Imperial Army had put Tanaka on their list of dangerous people and his personal safety outside Japan could not be assured. The Imperial Army commander in French Indochina then was Lieutenant Colonel Chō Isamu of the violent right-wing Sakurakai who was known to kill people he did not like (Tanaka 1961, p. 72). Tanaka was able to travel to China later in 1943 on an official mission of law professors to survey Chinese commercial customs. The group was led by his Law Faculty colleague Suehiro Izutarō who had been one of his harshest critics in the Hiraga Purge that had cost him the deanship. Not surprisingly, Suehiro was still displeased with Tanaka, complaining that he spent too much time in China talking about the Natural Law. Tanaka's point, expressed in an essay he published on Chinese commercial customs, was that the Natural Law had applicability in China too—a none-too-subtle jab at the militarists and others who were complicit in the violation of human rights in China.[9]

Tanaka fought the militarists and their supporters even within his own Faculty of Law at the Imperial University, the same faculty that had driven him out of the deanship back in 1939. This time it was over the promotion of Yasui Kaoru in late 1943. Tanaka and his colleague Yokota Kisaburō were strongly opposed to the promotion of Yasui on various grounds, including insufficient scholarly merit. There were procedural issues as well, since Yokota was Yasui's immediate supervisor in the field of international law and his negative recommendation was simply pushed aside by the Law Faculty Dean Suehiro who scheduled the motion for a full faculty vote. Tanaka and Yokota made the rounds to their colleagues, imploring them not to promote Yasui. Tanaka argued that Yasui was simply the militarists' candidate and would never have even been considered for promotion were it not for his collaboration with the militarists. When the faculty vote was counted, and Yasui was promoted by a two to one majority, Tanaka felt stabbed in the back by his colleagues, especially by

Nambara, Wagatsuma Sakae and Miyazawa Toshiyoshi (Maruyama and Fukuda 1989, p. 224). Tanaka and Yokota submitted their resignations in protest, but three months later, after entreaties from the junior faculty, including Maruyama Masao, they reconsidered in light of the vulnerable position their absence would put their junior colleagues and students in (Yanagisawa 1997, p. 80; Matsuzawa and Uete 2006, pp. 76–77). The Yasui affair was a complex matter, but one cannot discount an element of retribution against Tanaka for his role in the Hiraga Purge. Certainly Tanaka felt the law faculty was no longer a hospitable place for him, and he was soon looking for alternative employment.

By late 1944, Tanaka was meeting every two weeks with seven other globalist intellectuals and politicians in an effort to find a way to bring the war to a speedy end. This group included Abe Yoshishige, Shiga Naoya, Watsuji Tetsurō, Yamamoto Yūzō, Tanigawa Tetsuzō, and Kase Toshikazu. The honorary chairman of the group was Nishida Kitarō, modern Japan's preeminent philosopher. Abe was headmaster of the elite First Higher School and had clashed with the military over their efforts to shorten the curriculum so as to acquire more conscripts. Shiga Naoya's name might be surprising as he is mainly known as an apolitical novelist. But as Shin'ichi Shibata has written, "being a nephew of Shiga Naokata, a close confident of [Prince and former Prime Minister] Konoe Fumimaro, and the brother-in-law of Matsumura Giichi, member of the House of Peers and one time director-general of the Police Bureau of the Ministry of Home Affairs, Shiga appeared to have been equipped with his own information network" (Shibata 2015, p. 114). Watsuji was a leading philosopher with close connections to Japanese Christians like Tanaka's friend Yoshimitsu Yoshihiko. Yamamoto was a novelist and playwright who had criticized the militarists for their censorship. Tanigawa, a student of Nishida Kitarō, was a philosopher who promoted the idea of world government as the best guarantee of world peace. And Kase was a fluent English speaker who had studied at Amherst and Harvard and was serving as Foreign Minister Shigemitsu Mamoru's private secretary (Kase was also the uncle of Yoko Ono). They starting meeting at Shigemitsu's villa where they discussed strategies for bringing about an early end to the war and to plan for the nature of the Japanese State after the war. After April 1945 when Shigemitsu resigned as foreign minister, they met at Shiga Naoya's residence, as well as at the Christian Maeda Tamon's residence in the Takanawa neighborhood of

Tokyo, and at Tanaka's father-in-law Matsumoto Jōji's residence in the Den'en Chōfu suburb of Tokyo. This group of globalists, known as the Sannenkai ("Three Year Society"; the name was taken from the neighborhood where Shigemitsu's villa was located), was not successful in bringing the war to an early end. But they were the core of an elite network that struggled down to the end of the war to promote globalist values. Their significance lasted beyond the war, as they became the basis for the postwar group of writers known by their journal *Kokoro* ("heart") that spread globalist values in the postwar years.

In May 1945, after Tanaka's home in Tokyo was burned down in an air raid, he moved in with his father-in-law Matsumoto in Den'en Chōfu. In his reminiscences, Tanaka noted that as the war took a turn for the worse, four or five trusted colleagues from the Imperial University of Tokyo Law Faculty split into groups and approached senior ministers and influential politicians to let their opinions be known about the war. They included, in addition to Tanaka himself, Takagi Yasaka, doyen of American Studies in Japan, Wagatsuma Sakae, and the new Dean of the Imperial University of Tokyo Law Faculty, Nambara Shigeru. All were representative of the globalist intellectuals in Japan, and Takagi, Tanaka, and Nambara were at one time all members of Uchimura's Non-Church Christian circle. Tanaka himself went with Dean Nambara to see Wakatsuki Reijirō in Ito, Shizuoka prefecture and talked with him for three hours about the war situation. Wakatsuki was prime minister of Japan from 1926–1927, but is mainly known for resisting the Japanese militarists' hardline position in the London Naval Conference of 1930. Tanaka and Nambara discovered to their dismay how little influence the senior statesmen now had. Tanaka also visited former Prime Minister Konoe Fumimaro, former Vice-Chair of the Privy Council Hara Yoshimichi, and Counselor to the Privy Council Izawa Takio in Karuizawa and Tokyo where they talked frankly about their concerns with the war situation.

Tanaka's resistance to the militarists and his battles with less principled colleagues at the Imperial University of Tokyo have their source in his jurisprudence that found a universal principle in the Natural Law and in its expression in World Law. Even among his Law Faculty colleagues who did not share his unyielding principles, some recognized Tanaka's character for what it was. Nambara, with whom Tanaka had a tense but generally respectful relationship, noted that Tanaka was the kind of person who "saw things through to the end. He was consistent with his own ideas and did not rely on others to tell him what a person is like, especially when making personnel judgments at the university, he went down one road to its end. His article of faith was to act according to what was right and what was wrong" (Nambara, in Maruyama and Fukuda 1989, p. 218). It is clear that Nambara found Tanaka's moral principles a nuisance, if not just annoying, in academic administration. There was also a personal reason for his distance from Tanaka: Tanaka had written a critical review of Nambara's book *The State and Religion* in March 1943, and Nambara had replied with a much longer, testier rebuttal that basically reduced their differences in political philosophy to their respective Catholic or Protestant beliefs (See Tanaka 1943; Nambara 1943a, b). In the end, it is the historian Mitani Ta'ichirō who best articulated the link between Tanaka's globalist principles and his resistance to the ascendant forces in wartime Japan:

> In essence, Tanaka's criticism of ultra-nationalism and fascism was directed at the perversion of Truth, which was the tendency to subordinate law to power, the tendency to measure the Absolute by the particular. Here, in this theorist of Natural Law, we find an example of true conviction. (Mitani 1988, p. 191)

Notes

1. Ralf Michaels has noted that "Zitelmann's theory of private international law has been proposed as a model for conflict of laws in globalization" by Thomas Decker in a 2004 German thesis. See Michaels (2005, p. 38).
2. On these advocates for the "liberal theory of nationalism" and their influence on early twentieth century Japanese understandings of the nation, see Doak (1998, 2007, pp. 15–23).
3. For both Barker and Tanaka, the solution rested on a concept of law that was not produced by and for a single nation-state. Tanaka endorsed Zimmern's distinction between "Nationality" and "Statehood" which he expressed as "*minzoku*" and "*kokka*" (Tanaka 1932b, p. 194).
4. Tanaka's term *banmin* is most frequently seen as the translation of the Latin *gentium* (people, nation), as in *ius gentium* (*banmin hō*), an early form of the Natural Law, or "the law of the peoples." He certainly draws from the concept of *ius gentium* here, but makes it explicit that his meaning is broader, conveying the sense of all the people in the world, or "human society" (*jinrui shakai*). See Tanaka (1934a, pp. 667–668). Hence, I render it here as the "world people."

5. Tanaka frequently cites the maxim *ubi societas ibi ius* often in both Japanese and Latin throughout his writings. He opens the current work with an explanation of the maxim. See Tanaka (1932b, p. 10).
6. See Tanaka (1932a) and Tanaka (1934b).
7. See my brief discussion of the complex debate over the *kokutai* in the mid-1930s in Doak (2007, pp. 109–113).
8. On Tanaka's informal diplomacy in Latin America, see Doak (2018).
9. On Tanaka's activities in China and his views on China and the Natural Law, see (Doak, forthcoming).

References

Anan, Seiichi. 1962. Some Trends of Legal Thought and Natural Law Study in Japan; Note. *Natural Law Forum*, paper 75 (January): 109–119.

Barker, Sir Ernest. 1927. *National Character and the Factors in Its Formation.* London: Methuen.

Doak, Kevin M. 1998. Culture, Ethnicity and the State in Early Twentieth Century Japan. In *Japan's Competing Modernities: Issues in Culture and Democracy*, ed. Sharon Minichiello, 1900–1930. Honolulu: University of Hawaii Press.

———. 2007. *A History of Nationalism in Modern Japan: Placing the People.* Leiden: Brill.

———. 2018. Kōtarō Tanaka (1890–1974) and Global International Relations. In *Modern Japanese Political Thought and International Relations*, eds. Felix Rösch and Atsuko Watanabe. London: Rowman Littlefield International.

———. (forthcoming). Confucianism and Catholicism in Mid-Twentieth Century Japan. In *Confucianism and Catholicism: Reinvigorating the Dialogue*, eds. P.J. Ivanhoe and Michael Slater. University of Notre Dame Press.

Hanzawa, Takamaro. 1993. *Kindai nihon no katorishizumu: shisōshi-teki kōsatsu.* Tokyo: Misuzu Shobō.

Marshall, Byron K. 1978. Academic Factionalism in Japan: The Case of the Tōdai Economics Department, 1919–1939. *Modern Asian Studies* 12 (4): 529–551.

Maruyama, Masao, and Fukuda Kan'ichi, eds. 1989. *Kikigaki Nambara Shigeru kaikoroku.* Tokyo: Tokyo Daigaku Shuppankai.

Matsuzawa, Hiroaki, and Uete Michiari (eds.). 2006. *Maruyama Masao kai-kodan*, vol. 2. Tokyo: Iwanami Shoten.

Michaels, Ralf. 2005. The Re-state-ment of Non-State Law: The State, Choice of Law, and the Challenge from Global Legal Pluralism. *Duke Law School Legal Studies Research Paper Series* 81 (September): 1–53.

Minoda, Muneki. 1938. Tanaka Kōtarō no sekai hō no riron. *Kokka to Daigaku*. Tokyo: Nihon Genri Sha; reprinted in Imada Erika, ed., *Minoda Muneki zen-shū*. Tokyo: Kashiwa Shobō (2004), volume 5, pp. 5–380.

Mitani, Ta'ichirō. 1988. *Futatsu no sengo: kenryoku to chishikijin*. Tokyo: Chikuma Shobō.

Mitchell, Richard H. 1976. *Thought Control in Prewar Japan*. Ithaca: Cornell University Press.

Morgan, Jason, Minoda Muneki, Suehiro Izutarō, and Tanaka Kōtarō. 2018. Catholic Critiques of Statism in Interwar Japan. *Logos: A Journal of Catholic Thought and Culture* 21 (3):35–66.

Nambara, Shigeru. 1943a. Katorishisumu to Purotesutantisumu (1): Tanaka Kōtarō kyōju no hihyō o yomite. *Kokka gakkai zasshi* 57 (8): 67–87.

———. 1943b. Katorishisumu to Purotesutantisumu (2). *Kokka gakkai zasshi* 57 (9): 67–97.

Shibasaki, Atsushi. 2015. *Kokusai kankei no shisōshi: gurōbaru kankei kenkyū no tame ni*. Tokyo: Iwanami Shoten.

Shibata, Shin'ichi. 2015. The Emperor as Organ Theory Incident. In *Fifteen Lectures on Showa Japan*, ed. Kiyotada Tsutsui. Tokyo: Japan Publishing Industry for Culture.

Tachibana, Takashi. 2005. Shukugaku no tateyakusha, Tanaka Kōtarō no shimen soka. *Bungei Shunjū* (January): 394–407.

Takamine, Sadako. 1974. Rakujitsu no kagayaki: Tanaka Kōtarō no omoide—kirisutosha to seiji. *Koe* (July); reprinted in Suzuki Takeo ed., *Tanaka Kōtarō: hito to gyōseki*. Tokyo: Yūhikaku, 458–462.

Takeuchi, Yō. 2001. *Daigaku to iu yamai*. Tokyo: Chūō Kōron Shinsha.

Tanaka, Kōtarō. 1930. "Kojinshugi-teki shūkyō no muryoku" (May 12, 1930; no original source noted); published in Tanaka Kōtarō, *Kyōyō to bunka no kiso* (Tokyo: Iwanami Shoten, 1937), pp. 603–606.

———. 1932a. Fasshizumu to katorishizumu. *Yomiuri Shimbun* (May 10), p. 4.

———. 1932b. *Sekai hō no riron,* volume one. Tokyo: Iwanami Shoten.

———. 1934a. *Sekai hō no riron,* volume three. Tokyo: Iwanami Shoten.

———. 1934b. "Nachizu-teki hōritsu rinen no shisōshi-teki bunseki oyobi hihan." *Chūō Kōron* (April 10); reprinted in Tanaka 1937, pp. 221–264.

———. 1935. "Katorishizumu to kokusuishugi to jiyūshugi: Tosaka Jun-shi to kotau." *Yomiuri Shimbun* (June 1), p. 10.

———. 1937. *Kyōyō to bunka no kiso*. Tokyo: Iwanami Shoten.

———. 1943. Nambara Shigeru kyōju cho *Kokka to Shūkyō*. *Kokka gakkai zasshi* 57 (5): 102–113.

———. 1948. Saihan jo. In *Sekai hō no riron,* volume one, reprint. Tokyo: Iwanami Shoten, 1973.

———. 1961. *Watakushi no rirekisho*. Tokyo: Shunjū Sha.

Tosaka, Jun. 1935. Katorikku to kōdōshugi: Tōdai kyōju Tanaka Kōtarō-shi ni tazuneru. *Yomiuri Shimbun* (May 31), p. 10.

Urabe, Keishi. 2004. Tōkyō teikoku daigaku ni okeru gakusei shisō mondai to gakunai kanri ni kansuru kenkyū. *Kyūshū Daigaku Daigakuin Kyōiku Kōsu Insei Ronbunshū* 4: 67–90.

Yanagisawa, Ken. 1997. *Ikite kita michi*. Tokyo: Ōzora Sha.

Yomiuri Shimbun. 1938. Orimo ori, kizokuin de Tanaka kyōju ga yaridama, kokutai meichō ni han su to Mimurodo-shi ga. February 2, p. 2.

Zimmern, Sir Alfred E. 1923. Nationalism and Internationalism. *Foreign Affairs* 1 (4 June 15): 115–126.

CHAPTER 4

A Globalist at Home

Abstract This chapter covers the short, but intense, period of the early Occupation (1945–1950) when Tanaka served as the Minister of Education and as a legislator in the House of Councillors. Unable to travel overseas, Tanaka focused on implementing globalist values domestically. One key battle ground in this respect was the reformation of Japanese education, and his role in drafting the Fundamental Law of Education was crucial. Tanaka's Catholic values were not always welcomed by the Supreme Command of the Allied Powers (SCAP) whose commander General MacArthur staffed key posts with Freemasons like himself. Tanaka continued his independent stance as a Diet member, becoming a central figure in the unaligned Rokufūkai association of legislators. In the Diet, Tanaka drew on his globalist values and experiences to resist legislation sponsored by SCAP, such as the Eugenics Protection Bill.

Keywords Education reform in postwar Japan · *jinkaku* · Nambara Shigeru · Fundamental Law of Education · Freemasonry in occupied Japan · Eugenics Protection Bill

The early postwar years marked a transformation in Tanaka Kōtarō's career from a university law professor to a publicly engaged man. In the span of five years, Tanaka became the only person in modern Japanese history to serve in all three branches of government: as Minister of

K. M. Doak, *Tanaka Kōtarō and World Law*, Global Political Thinkers,
https://doi.org/10.1007/978-3-030-02035-4_4

Education in 1946, as a Diet member from 1947 to 1950, and as the Chief Justice of the Japanese Supreme Court from 1950 to 1960. These influential positions gave Tanaka unparalleled opportunities to promote his globalist values in Japan. While he never abandoned his interest in foreign travel, it must be remembered that foreign travel was all but impossible between 1945 and 1949 when Japan was under foreign military occupation and its currency was not exchangeable on the world market. Only when the yen was exchangeable at the rate of 360 yen to the US dollar on April 25, 1949 was foreign travel possible for Japanese citizens. Now, in theory, Japanese who had sufficient means could travel overseas. But in light of the rampant inflation and, more importantly, the fact that it was illegal to take foreign currency outside Japan and that Occupied Japan did not have the authority to issue passports (Watanabe 2002, pp. 115, 125, n. 19), as a practical matter, any Japanese who wished to travel overseas during the Occupation had to secure foreign sponsorship and financial support for the experience, as Tanaka finally did for his first overseas trip in postwar Japan to the United States in September of 1950. However, the lack of opportunity to travel overseas did not mean that Japanese people were uninterested in the broader world. In fact, there was wide coverage of, and great interest in, foreign culture (particularly in all things Western) in the popular journals and magazines. Tanaka was one of the most prolific publicists during the Occupation period and, as he left the academy, his globalist values also found fertile soil in education policy, politics and the judiciary.

The end of Tanaka's career as a law professor had its origins in the late wartime and immediate postwar years. We saw above in Chapter 3 that the Yasui Kaoru incident of 1943, following the Hiraga Purge of 1939, had alienated Tanaka from most of his Law Faculty colleagues. While he maintained an alliance against the war with his Protestant colleague Nambara Shigeru, their personal relationship had suffered from these academic battles and from a critical review Tanaka had written of Nambara's book in 1943. Nambara had become dean of the Imperial University of Tokyo Law Faculty in March 1945 and in December was elevated to president of the university. In addition to these push factors, there were also factors pulling Tanaka out of the university. In the final years of the war, Tanaka had worked with a group of globalist intellectuals called the Sannenkai to plan for a new Japan after the war. One of the Sannenkai members was Maeda Tamon. Shortly after Maeda was appointed Minister of Education under Prime Minister Higashikuni on August 18, 1945, he encouraged Tanaka to join him in the Ministry of Education as Chief of the Bureau of Schools and Education, a post created just for him. Tanaka found the offer irresistible, in part because of his good relations with Maeda, a fellow Christian, and in part because he already had several friends working in the Ministry of Education who were influenced by Christianity, including Yamasaki Kyōsuke (Tadasuke) and Sekiguchi Tai.[1] But his overriding consideration was the belief that he could finally achieve something through this government post that he had long wanted to do. This was "to sweep away the militaristic, extreme Statist educational ideal, to establish an independent right to education (that is, to liberate education both in the cities and in the countryside from the control of the bureaucrats), to undertake a fundamental reform of the normal schools which suffered from so many problems, and to improve the treatment of educators" (Tanaka 1961, p. 74). So, in October 1945 Tanaka became the Chief of the Bureau of Schools and Education first under Minister of Education Maeda and then under Abe Yoshishige, another member of the Sannenkai who served as Minister of Education from January to May 1946.

Education, particularly moral education, was a central concern for the Japanese (and for the Occupation officials), as there was a broad consensus in postwar society that better education was the key to preventing the kind of militarism that had engulfed Japan during the wartime. Remarkably, this push for moral education extended to lecturing Emperor Hirohito and his family on religions other than Shinto. In early March 1946, Bureau Chief Tanaka was visited by former Admiral Yamanashi Katsunoshin, President of Gakushūin University ("The Peers' University"), who invited him to give a lecture to the Imperial family on Catholicism. Daisetsu Suzuki was to give a lecture on Buddhism, and Professor Saitō Takeshi of the Imperial University of Tokyo was to lecture on Protestant Christianity (Kagawa Toyohiko had already given a lecture to the Emperor in January on Protestant Christianity). Tanaka gave his lecture at the Imperial Palace on April 30. Later published as "An Introduction to Catholicism," the lecture was quite clear on the difference between Protestantism (which Tanaka had embraced in his youth) and Catholicism. Addressing the topic of "Catholicism's contemporary mission," Tanaka made the following remarks to the Emperor that illustrate his globalist approach to moral education:

> The decadence in our present national morality of which we are so painfully aware should not be blamed on Western civilization itself. Extreme nationalists and Orientalists say that what polluted Japan was essentially the ideology of individualism in Western civilization which they take to be a material civilization. But this mistake comes from their equating Western civilization with either Western technological civilization or with Protestantism. We in Japan have only learned technological civilization or individualist ideology from the West; we have completely ignored traditional, spiritual Christian civilization. And we have not given enough thought to Oriental morality or to our own ancient Japanese good morals and laudable customs (*junpū bizoku*) which are part of the Natural Law. We merely discarded them as relics of feudalism. So, when we see that all we learned from the West was technological civilization and individualism (which was really egoism), we have to say that the decadence of our present national morality was simply inevitable. (Tanaka 1949b, pp. 63–64)

Here we see that Tanaka's globalism neither rejected aspects of non-Western moral traditions nor did it uncritically uphold all aspects of Western civilization and thought. He was neither an Orientalist nor an Occidentalist. He was a globalist. As he had for decades, he emphasized the need to discover the Truth as a universal principle, one applicable to all cultures. In the final lines of his lecture, he brought the point home: "Because Christian morality is grounded in the Natural Law, by no means does it contradict the morality of Japan or the Orient. It perfects the morality of Japan and the Orient by raising them up to the supernatural position of Christianity, thus internalizing and spiritualizing them. There it produces true spiritual understanding and piety in both East and West, indeed among all the peoples of the world, and thus builds up a foundation for world peace" (Tanaka 1949b, pp. 66–67). A better summary of Tanaka's globalism in religion would be hard to find.

Ironically, as Tanaka became increasingly involved in setting educational policy for postwar Japan, he necessarily was moving further from the possibility of retaining his position on the faculty of the Imperial University of Tokyo. When the Shidehara Cabinet resigned in May 1946, taking with it his friend Abe Yoshishige as Minister of Education, Tanaka believed he finally could leave government and return to the university. He did not know at the time that Abe had recommended him to incoming Prime Minister Yoshida Shigeru as a candidate for the next Minister of Education. When Yoshida offered the position to Tanaka, he readily agreed in the hopes of completing the work he had been undertaking in the Ministry. But he could no longer be an employee of a university that he, as Minister of Education, oversaw. The work in education he wanted to complete had its origins in his prewar jurisprudence where he had built on Jacques Maritain's concept of "the person" as distinct from "the individual." As Araki Shin'ichirō has demonstrated, Tanaka's focus on the person, and especially his influence from Maritain's idea that the goal of education was the "perfection of the person" (*jinkaku no kansei*), was deeply rooted in his study of the Natural Law and Catholic moral philosophy in general (Araki 2012, pp. 115–119, 136–138). Tanaka had a long track record in writing that the purpose of education was the "perfection of the person," and he had resisted militarist and nationalist influences in education as far back as the 1930s for that very reason. His anti-militarism and Christian values surely made him seem an attractive candidate for Minister of Education to the Supreme Command of the Allied Powers (SCAP) that oversaw the occupation of Japan.

Shortly after becoming Minister of Education, Tanaka found out that, in spite of Prime Minister Yoshida's support, he was not universally welcomed as a player in postwar education reform. On May 27, only five days after Tanaka's appointment, Nambara Shigeru reported to Deputy Chief Joseph Trainor of the Civil Information and Education (CIE) section of SCAP that he did not trust Tanaka who should be forced to recognize the superior authority of a committee of Japanese educators that Nambara chaired. On August 10 Nambara's committee was removed from the Ministry of Education and placed directly under the Prime Minister's Office, now renamed the Japan Education Reform Committee (JERC). In actuality, JERC worked closely with CIE, as Nambara was on particularly good terms with Mark Taylor Orr who in June was appointed Chief of the Education Division of CIE. As Minister of Education, Tanaka reported directly to CIE Section Chief Lieutenant Colonel Donald M. Nugent. Throughout Tanaka's tenure as Minister of Education, these struggles continued, with Nambara and CIE forging increasingly close relations, as Tanaka and the Ministry of Education suffered a corresponding loss of influence. Eventually a structure emerged of opposition from CIE/JERC against Tanaka and his Ministry of Education. Several issues shaped the conflict. Most importantly, Tanaka believed from his Natural Law perspective that the prewar Imperial Rescript on Education was a good moral influence for postwar education; Nambara and CIE did not (Araki 2004, pp. 4–5, 14). Secondly, CIE promoted a reorganization of lower education along the lines of the 6-3-3 system (six years of elementary, three years of middle school, and three years of high school). While Tanaka himself favored the 6-3-3 system, no one else at the senior level in his Ministry did. And finally, Tanaka was deeply concerned with the growing influence of Communism, especially within the Nikkyōso teachers union. SCAP was not yet interested in purging Communists from office, and when Tanaka relayed his concerns to Nugent, he was told not to worry about the Communists. Tanaka concluded that the Americans were naïve. Indeed, after the threatened General Strike in February 1947, General Douglas MacArthur, head of SCAP, changed his tune (Tanaka 1961, p. 78). But by then, Tanaka was no longer Minister of Education.

On Sunday afternoon May 5, 1946, while he was still Chief of the Bureau of Schools in the Ministry of Education, Tanaka joined Justice John P. Higgins (Chief Justice of the Massachusetts State Supreme Court and an American member of the International Military Tribunal of the Far East) at an Extension Lecture Series at Sophia University. Tanaka spoke on "Japan in the World." He laid out in clear terms his vision for postwar Japan as a true member nation of the world, something he argued Japan had never achieved yet. The solution was, as always, a moral one. And for Tanaka this meant recognizing that the Natural Law was the only bridge between the different cultures of East and West. In the published version of the lecture, Tanaka wrote that:

> Orientals, including the Japanese, are in and of themselves people of the Natural Law. It is this Natural Law that constitutes a common spiritual bond that can bring together the cultures of East and West. And raising this Natural Law to a supernatural level is the noble mission of Catholicism … . The faith that brings to Christian completion our national morality—this is what will give a reborn Japan the right to be a member of the community of nations and what will make us conscious for the first time in Japanese history of the position and mission of Japan in the world. It also, as a spiritual bond between East and West, will provide a firm foundation for world peace. (Tanaka 1946, p. 230)

The following month, Tanaka made similar remarks in the National Diet when he was asked by Diet members about his educational plans. On June 25, 1946, he said to the assembly that "true democratic education serves nothing but the truth; it must be thoroughly based on a recognition of the truth, a respect for the truth, and a love for the truth.

I believe that what must fill the vacuum left behind after we have swept away all the militarist and extreme nationalist materials from the content of education must be personalist education (*jinkaku kyōiku*) in the true sense" (Tanaka, cited in Araki 1997, p. 9). And he did not shy away from asserting that this personalist education had to have a religious sensibility to it. He was not proposing that Catholic or even Christian education be mandated by the State. But he argued that it was secular education in the prewar period that had allowed the dominance of nationalism and militarism, as the Japanese people had not been taught to seek sources of the truth independent of the State. As he concluded in comments before the Diet on August 16, "we are painfully aware that there is no more effective and thorough a method of saving ourselves from the moral decadence that is now running rampant in our State and society in the aftermath of our overcoming past ethnocentrism and egocentrism than to permeate our education at its very foundation with an education that has religious sensibility" (Tanaka, cited in Araki 2004, p. 14).

A critical moment in Tanaka's tenure as Minister of Education came on September 4, 1946. A summit meeting was held that evening for two hours between the Ministry of Education (Tanaka, Yamazaki Kyōsuke, Teranishi, translator), CIE (Nugent, Orr, Summers) and JERC (Abe Yoshishige, Nambara Shigeru) in the Tokyo Broadcasting Hall. This meeting between these three key educational organizations and the establishment of their respective lines of authority and responsibilities has been recognized for its "great significance in the history of postwar education" in Japan (Araki 2004, p. 9). At that meeting, CIE was able to establish two of its key priorities for postwar educational reform. First, the guarantee of the autonomy of JERC from Ministry control, and the ability of CIE to control the Ministry through the establishment of a steering committee. Araki Shin'ichirō has carefully studied the records of the summit meeting and notes that what was really at stake was not "reformists" (CIE/JERC) versus "conservatives" (the Ministry of Education). Rather, he points out that what Tanaka and Yamazaki wanted was "the best possible plan" and their Ministry was not trying to prevent the autonomous functioning of JERC. But arriving at the "best possible plan" was frustrated by divergent understandings of what the "best" was. Nambara (through Orr) argued that JERC should set the basic principles and the Ministry would merely apply those principles to the details. Tanaka replied that it was not easy to distinguish between basic principles and details, a position that Araki has shown was rooted in his support for the Natural Law as the "best" basic principle of all cultural policy and one that Nambara did not accept. Tanaka believed that if Truth itself were not the sovereign principle governing educational reform (for example, if the guiding principle were extreme individualism, as CIE insisted, or liberalism, as Nambara wanted), then it would result in a relativism of values that would invite the collapse of society. Araki is quite right to conclude that the argument over the independence of educational rights between Tanaka and the CIE really came down to the question of whether or not one adopted a position of truth-centered Man as Tanaka did. But there was another over-arching irony. Tanaka was arguing that the war experience taught the importance of the independence of education from the State in order to achieve the fundamental goal of education as the "perfection of the person" (*jinkaku no kansei*) (Araki 2004, pp. 11–15). But in 1946, it was the American State, and its allies like Nambara, who wanted to use the power of the State to establish the kind of education that they deemed best. To Tanaka, this looked like the same basic mistake of Japan's educational policy during the war.

Concerned that both CIE and JERC would carry out educational reform in a manner that would not establish the fundamental right to an education that serves the interests of the person rather than the State, Tanaka set the Ministry to the task of drafting an Outline for the Basic Law of Education. The Outline was hammered out between September 25 and November 29, and in the process Tanaka's most important phrase for educational reform, "the perfection of the person" (*jinkaku no kansei*) temporarily was removed and replaced with "humanity" (*ningensei*). To be fair, Tanaka was not the only person involved in postwar educational reform who was committed to the idea of "the person/personality" as the goal of education.[2] But he is generally recognized as having fiercely promoted the concept as the center of the postwar Fundamental Law of Education, fighting constantly to reinsert it into the law, which ultimately he did successfully (Araki 2005, pp. 1–2). The final version of the Fundamental Law of Education, passed on March 31, 1947 after Tanaka had stepped down as Minister of Education, nonetheless reflects Tanaka's key ideas in several places, but nowhere more so than in "Article One: The Aims of Education," which reads "Education shall aim for full development of personality [*jinkaku no kansei*= "the perfection of the person"] and strive to nurture the citizens, sound in mind and body, who are imbued with the qualities necessary for those who form a peaceful and democratic state and society."[3] This principle, still enshrined in law, that the goal of education is the perfection of the person is the greatest legacy Tanaka left from his short term as Minister of Education. Another legacy he left is the fact that, since the new Constitution was promulgated on November 3, 1946 (it went to effect May 3, 1947) while Tanaka was still Minister of Education, his signature is on the Constitution as a member of Prime Minister Yoshida's cabinet. This is a symbolic, but fitting, tribute to Tanaka since, as one of Japan's leading jurists, he always maintained that the postwar Constitution was based on the principles of the Natural Law.

Tanaka's difficulties and Nambara's relative success in working with the American Occupation can be explained also when their religious differences are taken into account—something often overlooked in the dominant narratives of postwar Japan that reflect secularist values. Nambara had defined their personal differences in the final years of the war as those of Protestantism versus Catholicism, in response to Tanaka's criticism of his book, *The State and Religion*. There is no question that Tanaka's values and politics came straight from his Catholic faith and particularly from his belief in the Natural Law. At first, his Christianity was appealing to SCAP officials who, under General MacArthur's directive, sought in general to Christianize postwar Japan. Some historians have emphasized MacArthur's ecumenical approach to Christianity, highlighting statements of gratitude from Catholics for MacArthur's largesse (Wittner 1971). A 2011 study by Tokumoto Eiichirō provides a different light, one that helps to explain why Protestants like Nambara fared much better under the Occupation than Catholics like Tanaka did. Tokumoto not only reminds us that MacArthur was a Freemason, but that he systematically promoted his fellow Freemasons to positions of influence in SCAP. As Tokumoto writes, "in the General Staff of GHQ back then, beginning with MacArthur at the top, high level Masons stood out" (Tokumoto 2011, p. 162). Among them were Robert Eichelberger, Walton H. Walker, Edward Mallory Almond, Charles A. Willoughby, Willliam F. Marquat, Courtney Whitney, Sidney L. Huff, Crawford F. Sams, Glen C. McBride, Abraham Jackobson, and Jack Napier. The influence of Masons was not merely in staffing, nor was it mere accident. Tokumoto notes that "MacArthur reflected Mason thinking throughout Occupation policy. To him that meant, not the building of Masonic lodges, but the change of the thinking of the Japanese people" (Tokumoto 2011, p. 269). His right hand man in this project was Major Michael A. Rivisto, a Thirty-Third Degree Freemason, who worked in the CIE and even tried to get the Emperor to become a Freemason. Broadly put, MacArthur and his fellow Masons promoted other Protestants in postwar Japan, most significantly the future Prime Minister Hatoyama Ichirō who was rehabilitated from a potential war criminal and inducted into the Freemasons in 1950 (and raised to a Third Degree Master Mason on March 26, 1955). Catholics of course were forbidden to join the Freemasons under penalty of excommunication. Indeed, one might even say that the main political lines in early postwar Japanese governance were between the Freemason Hatoyama and the (future) Catholic Yoshida Shigeru who represented not only the interests of the Catholic Church in Japan, but also the inclinations of the Emperor himself which were more aligned with Catholicism than Protestantism. Not surprisingly, Yoshida and Nambara did not get along, with Yoshida famously calling Nambara "one of those thugs who pervert scholarship to curry favor with the world" (*kyokugaku asei no to*).[4] But with Hatoyama's rehabilitation, Yoshida's political days were numbered and in late 1954, Hatoyama took the reins of government from Yoshida.

When Yoshida reshuffled his cabinet late in January 1947, he asked Tanaka to step aside as Minister of Education. Scholars have since debated the reason for Tanaka's dismissal (see Wray 1983, pp. 102–104). The most popular theory is that he was a sacrificial victim over the 6-3-3 system (Finn 1992, p. 133), an ironic turn of events since Tanaka personally supported the 6-3-3 reform. Tanaka himself believed that he was let go because Yoshida needed to save his government as SCAP was leaning to the left at the time and therefore he wanted to bring into his cabinet more people who were friendly to the socialists (Tanaka 1961, pp. 80–81). Tanaka was well-known as an implacable foe of Communism from prewar days. There may be elements of truth in all these views. But we should not overlook the tensions noted above between Tanaka and his Catholic and Natural Law values, on the one side, and the Protestant and relativist values of Nambara and SCAP on the other side. The new Minister of Education Takahashi Seiichirō is noted for three things: sharing Tanaka's belief that the Imperial Rescript on Education was not in conflict with the Fundamental Law of Education; passing the Fundamental Law of Education without change from Tanaka's draft; and being one of the few early postwar Ministers of Education who was not a Christian. He lasted a little over three months before Yoshida's government fell. Since Tanaka had to resign his position on the faculty of the

Imperial University of Tokyo when he became Minister of Education, he found himself facing unemployment in early 1947. Those close to him believed that he did not return to the Imperial University because Nambara never invited him back (see the comments of Yokota Kisaburō and Sagara Iichi in Suzuki 1977, p. 612). Having had a taste of political life, Tanaka decided to throw his hat in the ring for election to the House of Councillors as a non-affiliated candidate. His appeal reached across partisan divides, as evidenced by the names of his key supporters: Abe Yoshishige, Koizumi Shinzō, Ashida Hitoshi, Inukai Takeru, Takano Iwasaburō, and Izawa Takio (Tanaka 1961, p. 82). Tanaka got the largest number of votes and was elected to a six year term (half of those elected in 1947, the first year under the new Constitution, were elected to a three year term).

On May 3, 1947, Tanaka joined the Rokufūkai ("Green Breeze Society") an association of non-partisan Councillors that, with 108 members, constituted the largest faction in the Upper House. Tanaka, along with Shimojō Yasumaro, Tokugawa Muneyoshi, Satō Naotake, Matsudaira Tsuneo and Yamamoto Yūzō, was a key member of the Rokufūkai (Takenaka 2010, p. 39). Perhaps the best way to understand what "non-partisan" meant in early postwar Japan was as an embrace of globalism rather than alignment with one of the two nations that, after 1947, were hidden forces behind the major Japanese political parties: the United States behind the Liberals and the Soviet Union behind the Socialist and Communist parties. To remain unaffiliated in the Diet under these conditions was a commitment to a globalist response that rejected the national partisanship of the emerging Cold War. The Socialist Party had taken the Lower House (and the government) and the Americans still ruled Japan through SCAP. Makihara Izuru's comment on Tanaka's motivation in running for office is adroit: "just as his reason for entering the Ministry of Education came from a sense of opposition to administrative officials that believed education should not be left to them, he also ran as a candidate for the House of Councillors from a sense of opposition to both the [Japanese] government and the GHQ" (Makihara 2012, p. 233). In October of that year, Tanaka drafted the platform for the Rokufūkai. He appealed to the spirit of the new constitution, to the avoidance of extreme rightist or leftist positions, and to a sense of the common good and an emphasis on the value of family and tradition. He later admitted that he took his inspiration for the Rokufūkai platform from the prewar German Centre (*Zentrum*) Party

(Tanaka 1961, p. 82). The German Centre Party was so heavily Catholic in membership and values that it is also known informally as the Catholic Centre Party of Germany. While Tanaka never hid his Catholic values, he also worked closely with non-Christian Diet members, especially Horikoshi Girō, a member of the Tenrikyō New Religion and Umehara Shinryū, a Buddhist monk (Sagara Iichi, in Suzuki 1977, pp. 598–599), both members of the Rokufūkai.

In his 1947 *Culture and the New Constitution*, Tanaka linked his globalism to his effort to rebuild Japan by reconstructing culture. He renewed his prewar argument that culture must be understood as having its own autonomy from the State, but repositioned it as the foundation of a postwar democratic Japan (Tanaka 1947, pp. 13–14). As he had argued in the prewar period, Tanaka noted that there are two types of cultural activities: one that is extremely rich in a universal human character; the other where ethnic and local characteristics are salient. He felt it was essential that these two be seen as distinct yet mutually compatible:

> The effort to make universal culture, that is, a culture based on universal, human, global culture, into something particular is as mistaken as the effort to make particular cultures, that is, local ethnic cultures, universal … . We need to strongly uphold the particularity of local cultures and ethnic cultures. But at the same time there must be within them a more universal cultural value than mere exoticism. Only when there is, can we expect a global understanding of ethnic cultures, a national and even global understanding of local cultures. In this way, particular cultures can establish themselves within global culture alongside universal, human culture. (Tanaka 1947, p. 16)

From this theoretical foundation in the complementarity of the local and global, and from his principle that culture must not be reduced to the political State, Tanaka outlined how politicians should establish policies on religion and education that would not compromise freedom of conscience and the basic human right to education. Throughout the work, Tanaka emphasized that the autonomy of culture from politics does not mean that the State should adopt a hands-off approach to culture. Rather, it was the duty of the modern State to be involved in cultural matters in the interest of public welfare. He cited from Article 25 of the new constitution ("all people shall have the right to maintain the minimum standards of wholesome and cultured living") to support his argument on the modern State's duty to ensure the cultural well-being of the people—without descending into the Statism of the prewar period that held that the State was omnipotent (*Staatsomnipotenz*) (Tanaka 1947, p. 116).

Tanaka practiced what he preached. His major battles during his three years in the Diet were over social and cultural issues: divorce, education, and eugenics. And he engaged them all from his consistent philosophy of globalist ethics that resisted both Japanese nationalists as well as partisans of either the Soviet or American side. On August 29, 1947, as the Chairman of the Committee on Education (the Committee on Culture had since been separated from his committee), Tanaka emphasized the urgent need for sufficient funding to keep alive the preliminary efforts to establish the 6-3-3 education system that had already started in April. He stressed that the "6-3 system was absolutely necessary for the democratization of Japanese education" and that "the expenses for carrying it out were not merely assistance from the State but something that as a matter of principle the State has an obligation to bear" (Tanaka, in House of Councillors, September 19, 1947a, p. 392). At the conclusion of Tanaka's report, the motion passed the House of Councillors unanimously.

Tanaka also achieved a partial victory in proposing a revision to the Civil Law concerning divorce. At stake was his requirement that the family courts ascertain whether there existed true agreement of the parties to a consensual (uncontested) divorce before granting it. Tanaka invoked globalist principles, arguing that it was necessary to correct the weaknesses in the Japanese Civil Code in light of "trends in divorce laws among the civilized nations of the world" and "ultimately, in order to protect the social position of wives." Japan's consensual divorce laws were being used overwhelmingly by men who wanted to leave their wives and were able to either intimidate or defraud their wives into a "consensual" divorce. Tanaka argued that "Japan's Civil Code, in terms of consensual divorce, recognizes a freedom that is nearly unparalleled among other civilized countries. There is nothing wrong with freedom. But when that freedom is merely a name, as in 'free divorce,' we should recognize that the ultimate reality here is compulsory divorce. This situation cannot be permitted today when, under the new constitution, we must wipe away all evil feudal customs and thoroughly implement the spirit of protection of women, especially the equality of men and women." In his conclusion, Tanaka noted that, while Japan had an unfavorable reputation in the world as the world's foremost "divorce country" and should rethink its attitudes toward divorce in the future, at present he was only offering a modest proposal that family courts ensure that "consensual divorces" were really consensual (Tanaka, in House of Councillors-Japan, November 22, 1947b, pp. 785–786). Tanaka's proposed revision was opposed by Sai Takeo of the Japan Socialist Party who argued that having courts ascertain the facts of a consensual divorce was a violation of the Constitution, and he suggested that judicial intervention would only protect the interests of a few cases of fraud at the inconvenience of the many real consensual cases. Oku Mumeo, one of the leaders of the feminist movement in Japan and a member of the Rokufūkai, rose to Tanaka's defense. She noted that in her work with women she had often seen cases where "consensual divorce" was in reality coercive divorce with devastating effects on the women. She also mentioned that it was at a gathering of American and Japanese lawyers in fall of 1946 when she first became aware of the strange new legal term called "consensual divorce" (*kyōgi rikon*) in Japan (Oku Mumeo, in House of Councillors-Japan, November 22, 1947b, p. 789). Tanaka's proposed revision to the Civil Code passed the House of Councillors by a vote of 102 to 75. But it failed in the lower house due to what Tanaka described as "political negotiations" (Tanaka 1961, p. 83). It is not clear what the nature of those political negotiations were, but it is worth recalling that the prime minister at the time was Katayama Tetsu, the head of the Japan Socialist Party, the party to which Tanaka's opponent Sai Takeo belonged.

The Socialists created one more battleground for Tanaka in the Diet. In December 1947 Japan Socialist Party members Fukuda Masako, Katō Shizue, and Ota Tenrei introduced a Eugenic Protection Bill that allowed for surgical sterilization of a woman (when she or a relative or spouse had a genetic disorder) and abortion under certain circumstances—neither of which required the consent of the woman—and birth control under the control of doctors, nurses and midwives. The Bill was designed to legalize contraception, eugenic sterilization and abortion. SCAP wanted broader support for the Bill, especially from non-socialist Diet members, so a revised bill, under Liberal Party member Taniguchi Yasaburō's sponsorship, was introduced to the House of Councillors in June 1948 (and passed then with little debate). In May 1949, Taniguchi sponsored a revision to the Eugenic Protection Law that extended legal abortions to cases where a pregnancy was deemed to harm the mother's health for "physical or economic reasons" (Norgren 2001, pp. 44–45). While at first SCAP adopted a behind-the-scenes approach to the sensitive issue of abortion and birth control, "many SCAP officials viewed efforts to legalize birth control and abortion favorably and did not prevent the Eugenic Protection Law from being passed" (Norgren 2001, p. 43). In fact, by 1949, under the guidance of Colonel Crawford F. Sams, Chief of Staff at the Public Health Section, "SCAP authorities shared the Japanese elite's view that legalizing abortion and birth control was necessary to control overpopulation, which in turn would help rebuild the economy and prevent a resurgence of militarism" (Norgren 2001, p. 43). Sams was, of course, one of the senior Freemasons mentioned above as close to MacArthur. Kozy Amemiya gets right to the point: "Sams implicitly supported the liberalization of abortion" (Amemiya 1993, p. 176). But ultimately, responsibility for all bills proposed in the Japanese Diet rested with General Courtney Whitney, Chief of the Government Section and one of MacArthur's most influential Freemasons.[5]

Once again, Tanaka rose to challenge both the Socialists and the SCAP policy makers. He stated explicitly that his opposition to the proposed revision and the original Eugenic Protection Law came not from personal religious reasons but from practical considerations.[6] First, he argued that abortion is extremely harmful, physically and psychologically, to the health of, among others, the pregnant woman who undergoes the procedure. Second, he called for consideration of the relationship of abortion to extra-marital affairs and the effects they have on marriage and the family. He referred to his prewar research on the experiments with companionate and trial marriages in "a foreign country" (the United States) which always were linked to the issue of limiting childbirth. He noted that birth control and abortion always increase dramatically the number of divorces and he specifically referred to America as an example. And he added they also lead inevitably to "the extremely unnatural" practice of sterilization. He referred to the Comstock Laws that arose in America to prohibit the kind of salacious publications that now were flooding the Japanese markets with explicit descriptions of birth control procedures. More telling was his warning that "it will be truly vexing if we take as our basic attitude that this kind of medical technology is merely the result of scientific progress and since we are a cultural nation we must adopt such things" (Tanaka, in House of Councillors-Japan, May 14, 1949, p. 454). Tanaka noted that the proof of being a "cultural nation" is knowing the difference between using and abusing scientific technology, and that the Japanese had not paid enough attention to that distinction yet. Raising the issue of euthanasia and suicide, he argued that the Eugenic Protection Law was premised on a misunderstanding of basic human rights as something alienable and disposable. He linked this rejection of basic human rights to the fascist and totalitarian ideology that held if a family were poor it should cut its numbers in half, and if a nation's population of 80,000,000 was too many, it should reduce it to 60,000,000. He was particularly outraged by the proposition that the State should enforce such things. He concluded by addressing head-on the warped globalism behind the pro-eugenics side:

> Even if you say there are examples of such things in foreign countries, they've now learned their lessons overseas. To say that only Japan must use such ghastly methods is to contravene the spirit of international justice and humanity. If these are things some foreign country is trying to push on Japan, then I believe we should resolutely fight from now on openly in the international courts on the basis of a broad concept of global humanity and justice (cries of, "give us freedom"). If we think we should cut the number of families because there are too many people, or we should cut the population because the population is too large, that is saying that Man exists for food. But food exists for Man. The country exists for Man. Man must not become the slave of food. It is to defend the dignity of the person (applause) that I rise here as an opponent of this bill. (Tanaka, in House of Councillors-Japan, May 14, 1949, p. 454)

Tanaka implicitly called out the American Occupation forces as behind the promotion of the revised Eugenic Protection Law. And, as we saw, he was right. In particular, Crawford Sams was behind the alliance between conservative (including Yoshida Shigeru) and socialist Diet members that made possible the strong support in the Diet for the revised Eugenic Protection Law. After Tanaka's speech, a statement in support of the proposed revision was given by Inoue Natsue, head of the Japan Nurses Association, who argued that, given widespread poverty in Japan, abortion was a necessarily evil to enable women to have "an enjoyable family life." President of the House of Councillors Matsudaira Tsuneo called for a standing vote and recognized those in favor to have the majority, and the revised Eugenics Protection Law passed.

Not deterred by this setback, and in spite of his busy schedule in the Diet, Tanaka continued his work as a public intellectual to propagate globalist values broadly across Japanese society. In 1948, he had published *Culture and Worldview*, and in February of that year, he published an important article in the widely read journal *Kaizō* on "The Lessons of History" which was republished in his 1949 collection of essays, *In Search of Peace and Truth*. "The Lessons of History" drew on Tanaka's expertise in Latin American history to draw a comparison between the Paraguayan War of 1864–1870, the bloodiest war in Latin American history, and Japan's recent disastrous war in the Asia-Pacific region. Tanaka was aware of historians who interpreted the Paraguayan war as an anti-imperialist war by a small nation, just as he was aware of Japanese historians who justified Japan's role in World War II in similar terms. Both, he concluded, were sadly mistaken. The lesson of both wars to him was about the rise of vainglorious and undisciplined militarists whose madness led to the near destruction of their nations. Japan "was miraculously stopped just short of Paraguay's fate. We must engrave on our hearts the foolishness and horror of war and never imitate the Paraguayans by in future years falling into an amnesia that would enshrine our war leaders in Japan's pantheon" (Tanaka 1949a, at p. 229). In the same article, he argued that in Latin America, as dictatorships and communism arose in the aftermath of the war, what saved some degree of social stability in that region was the fact that Catholicism had permeated society. In Japan, however, the danger of communist dictatorship was much greater since among the ordinary Japanese people the "moral and cultural standards of the world and of the general intellectual class were not as high as in Latin America" (Tanaka 1949a, p. 229).

Indeed, in 1949 Japan the possibility of a communist take-over of society was not as absurd as it may seem today in retrospect. Internationally, Mao's Communist Party had just secured the Chinese mainland, and the Soviet Union successfully exploded its first atomic bomb. Domestically, the Japan Communist Party won an unprecedented ten per cent of the national vote, sending thirty-five Communist Party members to the Diet. The concern over communist influences in Japan had already sparked what some historians call "the reverse course" in SCAP policy at some point between 1947 and 1948 and it continued for the duration of the Occupation. Tanaka was certainly not alone in this concern. But his prescription was unusual.

For Tanaka, the battle between workers and capitalists was not about "bread." At its deepest level, it was a failure to understand and embrace global standards of morality. In a chapter originally published in the journal *Global Culture* in March 1948 and republished the following year in his book *Catholicism and the Contemporary Moment*, Tanaka argued that the best prospects for peaceful resolution of labor-capital strife and for peace in the world were found in the universal principles of morality best articulated in the Catholic tradition. "Communism's claim that morality differs by class," he noted, "makes the same mistake as fascism's claim that morality differs by *Volk* (*minzoku*). Both have in common a refusal to recognize moral principles that are universally valid for all mankind" (Tanaka 1949b, p. 116). Without an acceptance of universal moral principles, efforts to reconcile conflicts, whether based on economic class or ethnicity, will always be perceived as partisan and fail. Tanaka introduced the main arguments of papal encyclicals, such as Leo XIII's *Rerum Novarum* (1891) and Pius XI's *Quadragesimo Anno* (1931) on the labor question, and Pius XII's *Summi Pontificatus* (1939) on world peace. He stressed that these documents were not technical theological matters for Catholics only, but represented the Church's long tradition of resolving universal human problems based on justice and love, or what Tanaka interpreted as the Natural Law and Christian charity. Tanaka was fully aware that the majority of the Japanese were not Christian and even those who were Protestant often held certain misunderstandings about Catholicism. To both groups, he argued that "to a Catholic, something is not false because it is old, nor is it true because it is new. Nor is something right because it belongs to one's nation, nor is something wrong because it comes from another nation. For a Catholic, the standard of judgment is merely whether or not something is in accord with objective truth" (Tanaka 1949b, p. 117). He linked his argument on Catholicism as offering universal moral principles that were necessary for the Japanese people to understand globalist political principles to the new Constitution, since the new Constitution was premised on "a universal human moral principle, that is, the Natural Law" (Tanaka 1949b, p. 124). He concluded by re-stating his concern that both the materialists' rejection of the spiritual nature of Man and the subjectivists' rejection of objective moral standards held in common the belief that "Man is the measure of all things." Such egocentrism merely invited a spiritual vacuum that would lead to a violent anti-ethical social order or even to a chaos and anarchy reminiscent of scenes from Dostoevsky's *Demons* ("The Possessed"), the Russian writer's masterful allegory of the effects of nihilism. Tanaka was certainly not wrong about the appeal and lethal effects of nihilism. On June 13, 1948, three months after Tanaka's article was published, Dazai Osamu, postwar Japan's most articulate spokesman for nihilism, drowned himself with his lover in a ditch near his house.

In March 1949, while still a Diet member, Tanaka was appointed a professor at Gakushūin University, presumably through the connections he had with President Yamanashi from his 1946 lecture to the Emperor. It is not clear whether he ever taught a class there, but if so, it was for no longer than one year. The appointment was, however, a sign that Tanaka still considered himself first of all an intellectual, rather than a politician, and that he still had much to say. And a good deal of what he had to say was that Japan needed more intellectuals to emerge from ordinary people. Taking up the topic of "the participation of the masses in culture," Tanaka argued that "while a prophet may not be able to return home, what makes him popular is that a man who comes out from the masses is able to motivate the masses … . Of course, I don't believe that politics should be practiced only by politicians. When it comes to basic human rights, or basic political rights and responsibilities, or even questions of taxation, the right of the masses to speak out on such matters is something we have acquired as the result of historical struggle. This shows that what we call politics is something that basically belongs to the masses" (Tanaka Kōtarō, in Inoki et al. 1949, p. 239). However, Tanaka also resisted the efforts by conservatives and Marxists to glorify the "masses" or the "common folk" as the basis of their nationalistic rejection of globalism. So, in addition to emphasizing the continued need for an education based on personalism that would create new intellectual leaders from among the ordinary Japanese people, he also recognized the traditionalism that many Japanese people still embraced and that stood in the way of the globalist reforms that he believed in. He said that while most of the social reforms were indeed carried out by SCAP or at least under its encouragement, they were "all completely fitting and appropriate to Japanese society" (Tanaka, in Inoki et al. 1949, p. 242). Tanaka's argument was premised on his rejection of cultural relativism in favor of a globalism that asked not the cultural origins of a policy but whether it was just. He preferred that these reforms come from the Japanese government itself. But, he noted:

> if you ask why the government was not able to carry out these reforms on its own, I believe you have to consider that the general masses and the political parties were against them … . What some call the general masses

> are, as you can see from the election results, not the kind of progressive thing that we like to think they are. And I believe we must say that at least in Japan today we no longer have a situation where the government authorities or those directly involved in politics are the ones blocking progress. (Tanaka, in Inoki et al. 1949, p. 243)

Maruyama Masao could only add in response, "certainly the election results show they [the masses] are conservative" (Maruyama, in Inoki et al. 1949, 243).

Notes

1. According to Sonoda Yoshiaki, Yamazaki Kyōsuke (Tadasuke) was a Christian whereas Sekiguchi Tai was merely influenced by the Christian educator Nitobe Inazō. Sonoda (2008, pp. 135–136, 231). For more biographical details on Sekiguchi, see Chapter 1.
2. Dufourmont makes a case that the Confucian Yasuoka Masahiro also was a proponent of the role of the person (*jinkaku*) in education (see Dufourmont 2011, pp. 98–118). It should be noted however that Dufourmont does not credit Yasuoka with the exact phrase *jinkaku no kansei*, which was Tanaka's signature (derived from Jacques Maritain).
3. Tanaka's phrase *jinkaku no kansei* ("the perfection of personhood") survived the December 22, 2006 revision of the Fundamental Law on Education, although the official English translation dilutes the point by rendering the phrase as "fully developing the individual character"—a translation Nambara would appreciate more than Tanaka would. See Ministry of Education (2006).
4. Wikipedia-Japan, "Nambara Shigeru." This incident happened on May 3, 1950 as Nambara was giving a speech against the peace treaty with the US that excluded the USSR.
5. Cf. AG 320 (18 Mar. 47) GS Staff Memorandum Number 29, "No proposed legislation, whether in the form of a bill or other act of government ... will be approved by any staff section without coordination with the Government Section." Supreme Commander for the Allied Powers, Government Section (1948), Appendix G: 8a (5), p. 800.
6. Norgren brushes off Tanaka's opposition to the Eugenics Law as coming from a "Catholic politician" who believed "abortion ... was therefore a sin against the God-given natural order" (Norgren 2001, p. 46). But Tanaka, in his Diet speech, never mentions Catholicism or God, and explicitly states that his opposition does not come from religious grounds.

References

Amemiya, Kozy Kazuko. 1993. The Road to Pro-choice Ideology in Japan: A Social History of the Contest Between the State and Individuals Over Abortion. Doctoral dissertation, University of California, San Diego. Ann Arbor, MI: UMI.

Araki, Shin'ichirō. 1997. Tanaka Kōtarō no kyōiku mokutekikan: 'shinri no tankyū to jinkaku no kansei' o chūshin ni. *Kyūshū sangyō daigaku kokusai bunka gakubu kiyō*, number 9, pp. 1–12.

———. 2004. Kyōiku kihon hō yōkōan no seiritsu katei to kyōiku kihon hō no rippō ito. *Junshin jimbun kenkyū*, number 10, pp. 1–18.

———. 2005. Tanaka Kōtarō no kyōiku mokutekikan no seiritsu: jinkaku no kansei o chūshin ni shite. *Sengo kyōikushi kenkyū* 19 (December): 1–13.

———. 2012. Tanaka Kōtarō no kyōiku mokutekikan seiritsu ni ataeta Jakku Maritan no eikyō. In *Katorikku shakai fukushi kenkyū*, vol. 12, ed. Nagasaki Junshin Daigaku Katorikku Shakai Fukushi Kenkyūjo, 93–151.

Dufourmont, Eddy. 2011. Yasuoka Masahiro: A Conservative Vision of the Postwar. In *Japan's Postwar*, ed. Michael Lucken, Anne Bayard-Sakai, and Emmanuel Lozerand. London and New York: Routledge.

Finn, Richard B. 1992. *Winners in Peace: MacArthur, Yoshida, and Postwar Japan*. Berkeley: University of California Press.

House of Councillors-Japan. 1947a. Sangiin kaigiroku number 31. *Kanpō gōgai* (September 19).

———. 1947b. Sangiin kaigiroku number 55. *Kanpō gōgai* (November 22).

———. 1949. Sangiin kaigiroku number 26. *Kanpō gōgai* (May 14).

Inoki, Masamichi, Tanaka Kōtarō and Maruyama Masao. 1949. Gendai shakai ni okeru taishū. *Seiki* (October); reprinted in Maruyama, Masao. 1998. *Maruyama Masao zadan* 1: 226–253. Tokyo: Iwanami Shoten.

Makihara, Izuru. 2012. 'Bubun shakai'to 'zōge no tō': Mibuchi Tadahiko to Tanaka Kōtarō. In *Seiji o ikiru: rekishi to gendai no tōshizu*, ed. Iio Jun, Karube Tadashi, and Makihara Izuru. Tokyo: Chūō Kōron Shinsha.

Ministry of Education, Culture, Sports, Science and Technology-Japan. 2006. Basic Act on Education. http://www.mext.go.jp/en/policy/education/lawandplan/title01/detail01/1373798.htm. Accessed 16 July 2018.

Norgren, Tiana. 2001. *Abortion Before Birth Control: The Politics of Reproduction in Postwar Japan*. Princeton and Oxford: Princeton University Press.

Sonoda, Yoshiaki. 2008. *Kakusareta kōshitsu jimmyaku: kenpō kyūjō wa kurisuchan ga tsukutta no ka!?* Tokyo: Kōdansha.

Supreme Commander for the Allied Powers, Government Section. 1948. *Political Reorientation of Japan, September 1945 to September 1948*. Washington, DC: U.S. Government Printing Office.

Suzuki, Takeo (ed.). 1977. *Tanaka Kōtarō: hito to gyōseki*. Tokyo: Yūhikaku.

Takenaka, Harukata. 2010. *Sangiin to wa nanika, chūkō sōsho series*. Tokyo: Chūō Kōron Shinsha.

Tanaka, Kōtarō. Sekai ni okeru nihon. *Bōrō* (July 1946); reprinted in Tanaka 1949b, pp. 220–230.

———. 1947. *Shin kenpō to bunka*. Tokyo: Kokuritsu Shoin.

———. 1949a. Rekishi no kyōkun. *Kaizō* (February); reprinted in *Shinri to heiwa o motomete*. Tokyo: Kōdansha (1949), pp. 202–229.

———. 1949b. *Katorishizumu to gendai*. Tokyo: Kōkyō Sha.

———. 1961. *Watakushi no rirekisho*. Tokyo: Shunjū Sha.

Tokumoto, Eiichirō. 2011. *1945 Nihon senryō: furīmeisun kimitsu bunsho ga akasu tainichi senryaku*. Tokyo: Shinchō Sha.

Watanabe, Kazutami. 2002. The Dissolution of Mythology: Two 'Postwars'. In *Confluences: Postwar Japan and France*, ed. Douglas Slaymaker. Ann Arbor: University of Michigan Press.

Wikipedia-Japan. Nambara Shigeru. https://ja.wikipedia.org/wiki/南原繁. Accessed 28 July 2018.

Wittner, Lawrence S. 1971. MacArthur and the Missionaries: God and Man in Occupied Japan. *Pacific Historical Review* 10 (1): pp. 77–98.

Wray, Harry. 1983. Review of Toshio Nishi, *Unconditional Democracy: Education and Politics in Occupied Japan, 1945–1952. Monumenta Nipponica* 38 (1): 102–104.

CHAPTER 5

A Globalist Judge, at Home and Abroad

Abstract Focusing on Tanaka's role as a judge, the chapter opens with his appointment as the Chief Justice of the Japanese Supreme Court in 1950 and ending with his 1970 retirement from the International Court of Justice in The Hague. The Tanaka Court heard some of the most important cases in modern Japanese history, but Tanaka's importance extended beyond the decisions of the court to his critical role in establishing the independence of the court from outside influence. Both in Tokyo and at The Hague, Tanaka put into practice the principles of World Law, thus bringing to fruition the promise inherent in his life-long globalist jurisprudence. The culmination of his implementation of World Law is his famous dissenting opinion in the South West Africa Case that is still held up today as an example of the relevance of Natural Law to the defense of human rights and the struggle against racism.

Keywords Japanese Supreme Court · Mibuchi Tadahiko · World peace International Court of Justice · South West Africa Case

Early in 1950, Prime Minister Yoshida Shigeru appointed Tanaka Kōtarō to replace Chief Justice Mibuchi Tadahiko who had reached the mandatory retirement age of 70 on March 3, 1950. The day after stepping down from the court, Mibuchi was baptized a Catholic. Some believe it was his Christian wife Shizu's influence that led to his conversion (Wikipedia-Japan, "Mibuchi Tadahiko"). But contemporary

K. M. Doak, *Tanaka Kōtarō and World Law*, Global Political Thinkers,
https://doi.org/10.1007/978-3-030-02035-4_5

newspapers say it was Tanaka's doing. The *Nippon Times*, the major English language newspaper in Japan at the time, wrote that "outgoing Chief Justice Tadahiko Mibuchi of the Supreme Court accepted the Catholic faith and was baptized at the Chief Justice's official residence in Wakamatsu-Cho, Shinjuku Ward Friday. Mr. Mibuchi's entry into the [sic] Catholicism was brought about by the earnest persuasion of his successor, Dr. Kotaro Tanaka" (*Nippon Times*, "Mibuchi Becomes Catholic," p. 3).[1] Regardless of who deserves the credit for Mibuchi's conversion, the very fact that major media in Japan believed Tanaka was responsible is a measure (even if an overly generous one) of how widely he was seen as an influential globalist in early postwar Japan.

Yoshida's first choice to replace Mibuchi was Koizumi Shinzō, another Christian and a relative of Tanaka. Attorney General Ueda Shunkichi asked Tanaka to persuade Koizumi to take the position, but Koizumi would not accept it. So, the offer came to Tanaka himself. Tanaka's appointment as the new Chief Justice was greeted enthusiastically by the *Nippon Times*. The March 1, 1950 edition led off its editorial page with an article that said "the appointment of Dr. Kotaro Tanaka as the new Chief Justice of the Supreme Court is a happy choice which augurs the sound growth and development of the judiciary into a strong pillar of Japan's new democratic society. The selection will doubtlessly meet the approval of the people … . He has travelled extensively abroad and has a world outlook all too uncommon among the Japanese. At the same time, he is an ardent advocate of international peace" (*Nippon Times*, "The New Chief Justice," p. 2). The Japanese language *Yomiuri* newspaper carried a large photograph of the new Chief Justice in Japanese dress surrounded by Tokyo's leading men of culture: the "tiger-hunter" Tokugawa Yoshichika, diplomat and poet Yanagisawa Takeshi (Ken), and Italian expert and music scholar Tanabe Hisao who were celebrating the new Chief Justice and "guardian of the constitution" by treating him to a bowl of the traditional *oshiruko* soup at Tokugawa's home. The *Yomiuri* journalist made sure to inform readers that Tanaka had not skipped Sunday Mass that morning (*Yomiuri Shimbun*, "Oshiruko to kenpō no bannin," p. 2). The *Asahi* newspaper also greeted the news of Tanaka's appointment as generally a good thing, and Sekiguchi Tai (Tanaka's friend and colleague from the Ministry of Education) wrote an article introducing him as "a man who insists on justice" (Sekiguchi 1950, p. 1). Also on the front page, the *Asahi* offered an editorial, "What We Are Looking for from the New Chief Justice" which noted that, with Japanese society divided between conservatives and progressives, the paper hoped Tanaka would find the right course between the two extremes (*Asahi Shimbun*, "Shasetsu," 1950b, p. 1). In a separate article on the same page, the *Asahi* noted that in the competition for the position that had come down to Tanaka and Mano Tsuyoshi, Tanaka's advantages included his strong reputation as an international man (*Asahi Shimbun*, "Isasaka ginen," 1950a, p. 1).

Since Japan was still under occupation, Tanaka had to present himself upon appointment as Chief Justice to General MacArthur. This was the first of three meetings Tanaka had with MacArthur (the third was in New York after MacArthur's retirement). Tanaka was impressed with MacArthur who greeted him warmly and voiced his strong support for judicial independence and his belief (shared by Tanaka) that a jury system was premature in Japan. The judiciary, MacArthur told him, had to lead the democratization of the people (Tanaka 1961, p. 103). Tanaka welcomed MacArthur's instructions, as his own goal was to strengthen the independence of the judiciary. He later reflected that "the reason I thought [being a Supreme Court judge] was meaningful, important work was because I felt there was a particular need to strengthen the power of the judiciary under democratic politics. It is a judge's mission to bring about justice and protect fundamental human rights, but to accomplish that mission a judge had to be independent, not only from the executive and legislative branches, but also from journalists, labor unions and all other kinds of social influence … . This was what animated me during the ten years I was on the Supreme Court" (Tanaka 1961, p. 86). Tanaka noted that unlike other developed countries where the chief justice could focus exclusively on judging, Japan's chief justice was responsible for a great many administrative duties: repletion of the court's budget, compensation for judges, remodeling the judicial offices, the training of judges, and so forth. These duties brought him constantly into social and political conflict where he discovered that "in Japan, the power of the courts was not sufficiently strong and one could not say the status of the court was all that high" (Tanaka 1961, p. 87).

There was no "honeymoon period" for Chief Justice Tanaka. Already waiting for him was the very complicated and unfinished Case of the Mistaken Judgment of the Supreme Court (*saikō saibansho gohan jiken*). The defense attorney for a man condemned to life in prison for murder appealed the conviction on technical grounds, and the appeals courts and ultimately the Supreme Court got enmeshed in differences about what the law mandated. On October 17, 1949, Chief Justice Mibuchi held a conference with the four Supreme Court justices involved in "the mistaken judgment" and he recommended they resign. They refused. The matter was leaked to the mass media and was even taken up in the Diet where Mibuchi was called to testify. He repeated his position that the four judges should resign. Mibuchi fell ill and then reached retirement age without resolving the problem. Tanaka called a conference of the Supreme Court judges on June 24, 1950 and the majority of the judges recommended the four judges involved in the error be fined 10,000 yen. Tanaka, along with two other judges, felt a reprimand was sufficient. The SCAP official in charge of legislative matters was Dr. Alfred C. Oppler who opined that by their very nature "judges cannot make mistakes" and that he could not understand the court's decision to fine the judges (Tanaka 1961, p. 94). When Tanaka visited the United States a few months later as part of a group led by Oppler, he found that U.S. Chief Justice Fred M. Vinson had heard about the case and asked Tanaka if it was true that a judge on the Japanese Supreme Court had been fined. Tanaka felt embarrassed by the cultural peculiarities of the Japanese Supreme Court and renewed his commitment to bring the Japanese judiciary up to global standards (Tanaka 1961, p. 94).

The Case of the Mistaken Judgment impressed upon Tanaka the urgent need to reform the judiciary so that, rebuilt on universal principles of jurisprudence, it could truly serve as an independent branch of government for the first time. This also meant sweeping away the prewar positivist understanding of law based on Japan's Compendium of Laws (*roppō zenshū*) and replacing it with a globalist understanding of the rule of law (Makihara 2012, pp. 213–217). Makihara Izuru captures the challenges facing Chief Justice Tanaka well:

> The period when Tanaka served as Chief Justice, from 1950 to 1960, was the time when the Supreme Court became established as a political institution. This was, however, also a process when, internationally, the Cold War between East and West intensified and Japan regained her independence through negotiations with the West and strengthened her alliance with America. Domestically, it was the time when the Liberal Democratic Party was established and the conservative parties, who steadily secured the majority in the Diet, came face-to-face with opposition movements in the streets. The Supreme Court had to protect its independence under these political conditions, both internationally and domestically. (Makihara 2012, p. 219)

As with so many other things during the 1950s, the Supreme Court also was divided: the Hosono Nagayoshi faction stood for greater judicial independence against the anti-Hosono faction. According to Suzuki Chūichi, Chief of the Personnel Division of the Supreme Court, Tanaka was able to succeed where Mibuchi had failed because in meetings with other judges he had "an attitude that was open to the opinions of other judges" (Suzuki Chūichi, cited in Makihara 2012, p. 220). This attitude stemmed from Tanaka's belief that institutions like the court should be understood as constituting in themselves independent societies in which each member has a specific role to play. Makihara lists three elements of Tanaka's effort to develop the Supreme Court as a "trans-political" judicial institution: (1) his recognition that the courts were relatively weak in the face of social and State influences; (2) his strong reliance on globalist education (*kyōyō*); and (3) his theoretical consistency in seeing the need during the wartime for greater independence of the universities from the Ministry of Education and, while serving in the postwar Diet and the Supreme Court, for greater independence of a person's right to education and of the judiciary (Makihara 2012, pp. 230–236). Makihara accurately locates the core of Tanaka's argument for the independent judiciary in his theory of "partial societies" that saw any single national society as composed of multiple overlapping societies that took priority over political organizations like the State. As we saw above in Chapter 3, this social theory was the very foundation of Tanaka's theory of World Law that recognized, not only "micro-societies" within Japan, but also the world as a global society and law as emanating, not from the State, but from society itself (*ubi societas ibi ius*).

In 1950, Tanaka finally got his first chance in the postwar period to travel overseas. Flying out of Haneda Airport on September 27, he was the most senior member of a group of Japanese jurists led by Dr. Oppler, Chief of the Courts and Law Division of the Government Section of SCAP, who had invited the Japanese jurists on a GARIOA (Government Aid and Relief in Occupied Areas) grant to study the American system of justice. As a sign of how highly SCAP regarded this mission, the group was addressed before departure by General Courtney Whitney, Chief of Government Section, and by Alva C. Carpenter, Chief of the Legal Section—General MacArthur had his hands full then with the Korean War (Tanaka 1953a, pp. 13–14).[2] And Charles L. Kades, Whitney's former Deputy Chief, was waiting for the mission in New York City where he provided substantial assistance to them (Tanaka 1953a, p. 20).

In addition to Tanaka, the group included Mano Tsuyoshi and Hozumi Shigetō from the Supreme Court, Iisaka Suichi, President of the Sendai High Court, Higuchi Masaru and Kishi Seiichi, judges of the Tokyo Higher Court and Nisei interpreter and lawyer George Koshi. As Tanaka later reflected, it was a useful trip for him, since his knowledge of the law was largely shaped by continental law, particularly German law, reflecting the bias of Japan's prewar legal system (Tanaka 1953a, p. 21). It was an intense experience, studying American technical legal terms and systems, visiting courts, universities and law offices, often getting no more than five hours of sleep per night over a period of forty-five days. Tanaka thought the pace was too much for the portly 67 year old Hozumi who fell ill soon after returning to Japan and died about six months later (Tanaka 1961, pp. 107–108).

While on the mission, Tanaka was awarded honorary doctorates from three Catholic universities: Boston College, Fordham University, and Georgetown University. In his speech on the occasion of receiving the honorary degree of Doctor of Laws from Georgetown University on October 29, he sounded the same notes that Makihara discerned in Tanaka's defense of the political independence of key social institutions. But in his speech, Tanaka made explicit the role of the Natural Law:

> What I have felt is, that in many respects, the problems we are confronting in this critical moment and the alternatives of solution are almost identical with yours and may say [sic] with the rest of the democratic world, that there is no prompt and perfect solution to these complicated problems.
>
> … The independence of universities not only from the government but from any other possible interference can be safe-guarded only when they are consecrated to the eternal and objective truth, to what God wishes to be.
>
> … Upon assuming my office in the Supreme Court of Japan, I have been thoroughly convinced of the theoretical identity between the autonomy of universities and the independence of the judiciary. With the same love and zeal I had served the university, I am firmly resolved to assume leadership in the Japanese judiciary, so that it really becomes the guardian of the new constitution of Japan, which is based on the principles of natural law. (Tanaka 1950, "Address")

It was a critical trip for Tanaka, as it provided him with a new, American element in his global jurisprudence. His first trip across America as a student on his way to Europe in 1919 had not left him with a favorable impression of American civilization. This time, with a much greater exposure to the concepts and institutions of American jurisprudence, he came away with an expanded understanding of globalism in jurisprudence. While his fundamental position based on the Natural Law had not changed, he now had first-hand experience of how the Natural Law could work with legal systems as different as the continental and Anglo-American ones. This understanding was very useful in the ongoing efforts to globalize the Japanese legal system in postwar Japan. But it is also important to note that, by publishing a book *Travels in America* in 1953 that detailed his experiences and thoughts while in America, Tanaka contributed to an enhanced global consciousness (in particular, a positive view of America) among his postwar Japanese readers.

Shortly after returning to Japan in early November, Tanaka drafted one of the most globalist of his articles that, at the same time, reflected his new appreciation for American democracy. "Peace and Justice" enjoyed a wide readership in both Japan and the United States. It was originally published in Japanese in the journal *Kokoro* in January 1951, then published in English in the *Nippon Times* on January 17, 1952, and reprinted in the *Catholic University Law Review* (January 1952) and in *The American Bar Association Journal* (August 1952). The article was a response to a challenge from Japanese leftists (for example, Nambara Shigeru) who protested against the San Francisco Peace Treaty and called for "peace at all costs." Tanaka's position was that Japan, as a newly independent nation under the San Francisco Peace Treaty, must "be faithful to the United Nations and UNESCO which are identical with the Japanese Constitution in spirit" (Tanaka 1952, p. 664). He noted that by signing the San Francisco Peace Treaty Japan had become a partisan in the postwar division of the world order; neutrality in the face of the evils of Communism was not an option, no matter how attractive peace might seem in the aftermath of the horrific Second World War. He held that "advocates of neutrality are ones who either fail to recognize or are skeptical of [the] distinction between justice and injustice and between good and evil or ones who, if they recognize it, possess no strong sense of justice and morality. None but relativists can be neutral between justice and injustice or between good and evil. And skeptics alone are capable of a compromising attitude toward both" (Tanaka 1952, pp. 664, 675). And he concluded that "at the present conjuncture nothing is more harmful than skepticism" (Tanaka 1952, p. 675).

After Japan regained independence in 1952, and with the resources his salary as Chief Justice provided (equal to the salary of the Prime Minister), Tanaka returned to his favorite activity, foreign travel. In July 1953 the American Bar Association invited him to its 76th General Meeting in Boston where Tanaka met many of the chief justices of American state supreme courts. On the return leg in September, he travelled through Canada. From January 21 to the middle of March 1956, he went on a world tour to India, the Dominican Republic, France and Italy as an official State guest in each country. It was his first visit to India (he spent twelve days there). It was also his first return to Europe in twenty years, so while there he also visited Switzerland, West Germany, and the United Kingdom. While in Rome, he went to the Vatican for an audience with Pope Pius XII. Three years earlier, the Pope had invested Tanaka as a Knight in the Order of St. Sylvester, the highest rank in the order given to lay Catholics for distinguishing themselves in the professions and the arts (Fig. 5.1).

Fig. 5.1 Mrs. Tanaka (nèe Matsumoto) Mineko, Pope Pius XII, and Tanaka Kōtarō, 1956 (image from Getty database)

On his return, Tanaka went through the United States, deepening his understanding of the American judicial system and visiting with old friends on the law faculties of Stanford and the University of California at Berkeley. The trip was a front page story in the *Nippon Times* which noted that this time his wife accompanied him (*Nippon Times*, "Chief Justice Going Abroad," 1956, p. 1). And in 1957, Tanaka spent the month of December traveling to Latin America. He was invited by Orozimbo Nonato da Silva, the Chief Justice of the Brazilian Supreme Federal Court, to attend their Judicial Day (which Tanaka established in Japan on his return). While there, he inspected their judicial system, gave lectures, and enjoyed reunions with many of his friends from his 1939 trip. On the trip, he also visited the United States, Venezuela, Panama, Guatemala and Mexico. As with his earlier trip to the United States, he wrote a book about his travels in Latin America called *From Brazil to Mexico*, replete with photos and reflections on the cultures he encountered there (Tanaka 1958a). This frequency of international travel was a privilege for anyone in 1950s Japan. But it is important to recognize that Tanaka did not keep his travels and cultural impressions private, but published his overseas experiences widely in the Japanese press. In so doing, he made a major contribution to raising global consciousness in postwar Japan, particularly during a time when few Japanese had the resources and opportunity to travel outside the country.

Of course, Tanaka's globalist writings were not limited to travelogues. One of the most widely read of his publications throughout the postwar period was an article he wrote in 1951 on "Law and the World." First published in a 1954 volume of his essays called *A Legal Philosophy for Peace*, it was republished in volume four of his *Collected Works* in 1960, and again in his *Sequel to A Theory of World Law* in 1972. His argument is both a product of its time and timeless. As a product of its time, it was a profound reflection on the tragedy of the Korean War following so soon after the end of World War II. But it transcended its time, both in going back to Tanaka's prewar argument in favor of a World Law and in setting out principles for world peace that stand the test of time. The basis of Tanaka's argument for World Law, as we saw in Chapter 3 above, was the classic maxim *ubi societas ibi ius* applied to the growing recognition of a world society formed through more frequent international commerce and transportation. The question of a permanent world peace then rested on the establishment of a true world community (Tanaka preferred the English term "world community" but in

Japanese used the words for "world society," *sekai shakai*). The reality of the Korean War demonstrated that, far from the unification of the world into one society or "world community" that he had long hoped for, the world in fact was deeply divided into two camps: one led by the United States and the other led by the Soviet Union, each with irreconcilable political ideals. Nationalism was also a factor working against world unity, and thus against world peace. His analysis of the situation, as usual, was adroit:

> It is precisely this kind of internationalizing of national political principles, especially the internationalization of common ideals, that forms a basic unity in the principles of domestic politics and international politics and that must become the foundation for the future of the international community and particularly for the realization of permanent world peace. (Tanaka 1954a, p. 89)

If there were any hope of forming a world community from the divided camps of the day, Tanaka believed that "the minimum condition" to be met was "unity behind the fundamental principles of democratic societies such as respect for law and order, a rejection of violence, the guarantee of basic human rights, and the realization of justice" (Tanaka 1954a, p. 91). He believed fervently in world peace, but he was not naïve. He saw clearly that these conditions had not yet been met, nor were they likely to be anytime soon. He envisioned a hard struggle ahead because "in most cases, peace must be fought for and sacrificed for. And to that extent, and because of that, peace is valued" (Tanaka 1954a, p. 92). Peace without justice was not a peace worth having. And justice was linked to the question of law. So the possibility of world peace was inseparable from the establishment of a true world society that would strengthen the already budding reality of a World Law. As Tanaka said in the conclusion to his article, "In other worlds, peace means order, and such an order is an expression of human nature correctly understood; it is none other than the rule of the universal Natural Law" (Tanaka 1954a, p. 92).

One of the unintended consequences of the democratization of postwar Japan was the unleashing of social forces that often did not understand the proper limits of popular democracy with respect to the administration of justice. Tanaka praised the new constitution for holding that "fundamental human rights were not created by the State. They are eternal and universal institutions, common to all mankind and antedating the State, and founded upon natural law (see the Preamble and Article 11)" (Tanaka 1953b, p. 5). Moreover, he noted that this enshrining of the Natural Law in the constitution, along with the right of the Supreme Court to overturn any positive law (regardless of how popular it might be) that was in violation of these natural rights, were new developments in postwar Japan. He accepted the new principle of popular sovereignty as a positive change, but he also understood as a judge that the people's rights were not unlimited. As he pointed out, "the people must refrain from an abuse of their rights and freedom, and are always to be responsible for utilizing them for the public welfare (Article 12). The public welfare is a growth from the natural character of a body politic called the State. It is the duty of the Supreme Court to determine the respective bounds of the two concepts through decision of concrete cases coming before it" (Tanaka 1953b, p. 5). Already in the early 1950s, there was a vigorous debate in Japan about whether the existence of the Self Defense Force violated Article 9 of the Constitution. Suzuki Mosaburō, Chairman of the Central Executive Committee of the Socialist Party, had asked the Supreme Court to find the law providing for the establishment of the National Police Reserve to be unconstitutional. On October 8, 1952 the full bench of the Supreme Court dismissed the request, noting that it had no power to make any such determination without a case that had worked its way up through the lower courts. They were not about to set aside legal procedure in order to turn the court into a political tool of populist sentiment.

The May 17, 1954 United States Supreme Court decision in Brown v. Board of Education that overturned the 1896 Plessy v. Ferguson decision renewed attention to the new power of the postwar Japanese Supreme Court to declare laws unconstitutional and to overturn earlier court judgments. Tanaka felt compelled to remind the public that, in contrast to the Supreme Court of West Germany, Japan's Supreme Court could not rule on the constitutionality of a law without a relevant case working its way up through the court system first. He considered respect for judicial order as essential to the protection of human rights. As he noted, "Article 31 of the Constitution speaks about 'procedure established by law' and judges wear out their nerves trying to stick to the letter of the troublesome rules about procedure in court and about litigation simply because if they were not respected the fundamental human rights are liable to be violated by arbitrary decisions on the part of the courts" (Tanaka 1954b, p. 8). At the same time, he worried about the backlog of cases (in the mid 1950s, his Supreme Court had nearly 6000 pending cases) and the tradition of Japanese judges not to put much emphasis on administrative efficiency. Making the courts more efficient and reducing the backlog was one of Chief Justice Tanaka's priorities. His recommendation, although long, merits citation here as it goes right to the heart of Tanaka's globalism as a judge (and it is presented in his own English):

> I should like to request our judicial branch to adopt a universal point of view about two things. In Japan, the administrative aspect of judicial proceedings has formerly been rather neglected, in contrast with jurisprudence, to which was accorded profound study. In the first place, therefore, we must be critical from the international view of what we are actually doing. Fortunately such an atmosphere is gradually forming in our country. Visits of jurists to and from Japan and America have become frequent since the end of the war, and quite a number of Japanese judges, procurators and lawyers have visited the United States; while there, they studied how the judicial business was managed in America, and on returning home they have provided a stimulus to the improvement of our judicial administration by their resulting suggestions. Such useful inspection-trips by jurists are recently being made not only to the United States but to England and other countries also. It is certain that the presence of Japanese delegates or observers at the international conference of jurists held in Berlin and Madrid last summer helped the Japanese legal profession to recognization of the universal nature of the mission of justice and to feeling keenly the necessity of coöperation of all nations for realization of their common object. Secondly, such coöperation of various nations, understanding the universality of the object of justice, will be possible only when they acknowledge the existence of a basic rule, universal for mankind, of human righteousness and freedom. This basic rule is nothing more than the Law of Nature. It is the ethical principle constituting the foundations of the charter of the United Nations and the Declaration of Universal Human Rights of 1948, and also of what is solemnly declared in our Constitution … . Mutual cooperation of all free nations in efforts to protect and realize the Law of Nature is an indistinguishable condition for democratization of the whole world, and for the lasting peace and welfare of humanity. The judicial branch of every country is shouldering in its area that universal duty. The mission of the Japanese judicial branch, too, is to discharge its own share in this universal duty. (Tanaka 1953b, pp. 13–14)

While this particular text was written in English and aimed at non-Japanese as part of a soft-power diplomacy initiative of the Ministry of Foreign Affairs, the message was not for Westerners only. Tanaka published the same basic argument, with greater elaboration, in a series of articles in Japanese throughout the decade: "On the Independence and Conscience of Judges" (1954); "The Court and Public Opinion" (1955), "The Court" (1955) and "The Courts and Freedom of the Press" (1958).[3] In addition to these academic articles, he maintained an impressive flow of publications in the major newspapers and journals, adjusting the level of argumentation appropriately for his audience.

During Tanaka's tenure as Chief Justice, the Japanese Supreme Court decided some of the most controversial cases in its history. Here I can only mention a few of the most significant. The *Lady Chatterly's Lover* Case arose when Koyama Books published Itō Sei's unabridged translation of D.H. Lawrence's novel and the publishing house's president Koyama Hisajirō was charged under Article 175 of the Penal Code that prohibited the publication of obscene material. The incident occurred in 1951 while Japan was still under occupation, so many were interested to see if Japan's own courts would rule consistently with the decision of the SCAP censors. After guilty verdicts in the lower courts in January and December of 1952 (the first court exonerated the translator, the second court found the translator also guilty but imposed a lighter fine on him than on the publisher), the case reached the Supreme Court. Already a diverse group of Japanese intellectuals had formed in support of the defendants and there was considerable pressure on the Supreme Court to overturn the lower courts' verdicts. It did not. On April 5, 1957, by a unanimous vote of 11-0, the Supreme Court confirmed the lower court's decision and ordered the publisher and translator to be fined in accordance with the law. In rendering its decision, the court said that the publication of obscene material harmed "the public welfare" (*kōkyō no fukushi*) (Supreme Court of Japan Decision in the Lady Chatterly's Lover Case 1957, pp. 9–11), a constitutional term very close to Chief Justice Tanaka's long-standing interest in "the common good." Two points in this respect reflect Tanaka's broader concerns for the specific role of the judiciary: one, whether it was the responsibility of the judiciary to decide what was in the interests of the public welfare; and two, what limitations, if any, the law could set on the expression of individual rights. The Court spoke unanimously in answer to those two issues, but it also did so in a broad, globalist consensus as courts around the world largely decided in a similar way on the publication of *Lady Chatterly's Lover* in their countries. Japan's Supreme Court decision in this case was more evidence of Japan's growing globalism in its jurisprudence.

Two other cases the Tanaka Court decided were even more controversial. The Matsukawa Case arose when a train derailed in the early morning hours of August 17, 1949 near the Matsukawa station in Fukushima Prefecture. Three crewmen were killed. It was the most notorious of three railroad-related incidents of 1949: the other two were the July 6 death and dismemberment of Shimoyama Sadayori, president of Japan National Railways, and the July 15 Mitaka incident where a runaway train killed six and injured twenty people at Mitaka station. Communist Party members were the bulk of the defendants in the Mitaka and Matsukawa cases; there was no arrest in the Shimoyama incident. In the Matsukawa Case, twenty people were arrested and all were convicted in the Fukushima District Court trial in 1950. At the appeal to the Sendai High Court in 1955, the defendants recanted their confessions. Seventeen of the twenty had their guilty verdicts confirmed. The writer Hirotsu Kazuo took up their case, publishing a long serialized essay in their defense in *Chūō Kōron*, a high profile journal, and soon many intellectuals joined the movement to have them acquitted. It became something like postwar Japan's version of *fin de siècle* France's Dreyfus Case. On October 5, 1958, as the Supreme Court was preparing for oral arguments in the Matsukawa Case, the *Yomiuri* newspaper carried a major story on 3500 letters, telegrams and phone calls that the Supreme Court had received about the case, many of them threatening the judges if they did not acquit the defendants. The story mentioned Justices Ikeda, Otani and Tanaka as personally singled out by the threatening letters. The one letter cited that was addressed to Tanaka read "give us justice! If you don't, you won't live much longer. If you don't give a verdict of not guilty, you'll see more of my perfect crimes!" (*Yomiuri Shimbun*, "Saikōsai e tōsho senjutsu," 1958, p. 11).[4] In its decision, the Supreme Court referred the Matsukawa Case back to the Sendai High Court for retrial by a vote of 7-5 (three judges were absent due to illness [Saitō, Kawamura] or recusal [Ishizaka]). Tanaka and three others voted that the appeal be rejected; one other colleague opined that the original verdict be set aside and the Supreme Court make its own decision. After the case was returned to Sendai, all defendants were found not guilty. The real perpetrator was never found and the case remains one of the great unsolved crimes in Japanese history. But it was Tanaka's May 1955 instruction to judges (while the case was working its way through the system) "not to listen to noise" (*zatsuon ni mimi o kasuna*) that inflamed social activists on the left who in fact had been making quite a lot of noise in order to influence the judges (*Yomiuri Shimbun*, "Kensei ya engekika," 1959, p. 5). At issue was whether the courts should respond to the demands of social movements or whether, as Tanaka believed, it was the duty of the court to resist external pressures and render judgments as judges saw fit, solely in accordance with the demands of the law. To Tanaka, the real question was the maturation of the courts as an independent, co-equal branch of government. The court was not the legislature where the people's desires should determine results (Tanaka 1961, pp. 120–121).

Without a doubt, the most controversial case Tanaka was involved in was the Sunakawa Case (Sakata v. Japan), a decision that is still discussed and even cited today by leading politicians, academics and others.[5] The Sunakawa Case had its origins in a series of military base protests that started in 1955. On July 8, 1957, some protestors broke into the American military base at Sunakawa. Seven of them were arrested and charged with trespassing. The Tokyo District Court found them not guilty, reasoning that the United States Japan Security Treaty was unconstitutional under Article 9 and thus the bases were illegal to begin with. On December 16, 1959, the Supreme Court unanimously overturned the District Court's decision and remanded the case back to the Tokyo District Court. In its reasoning, the Supreme Court held that "unless the said treaty is obviously unconstitutional and void, it falls outside the purview of the power of judicial review granted to the court" ("Sakata *v.* Japan (The Sunakawa Case) ," p. 163). By merely pointing out that the forces at the base were foreign troops not under Japanese control, the court easily noted that they were not an obvious contradiction to Article 9. But the Supreme Court's decision also reflected Tanaka's globalism in declaring that the Constitution shows that the Japanese people "have determined to supplement the shortcomings in our national defense resulting [from Article 9] … by trusting in the justice and faith of the peace loving people of the world, and thereby preserve our peace and existence" (Supreme Court of Japan, "Judgment upon case of the so-called 'SUNAKAWA CASE'"). In an article he wrote in English five years later, Tanaka reflected that one of the important points of the Sunakawa Case was determining how the Court would regard treaties. He noted that while a few of the judges felt that the Court could rule on the constitutionality of treaties, the majority felt that "self-restraint on matters of a highly political nature is essential to the independence of the courts" (Tanaka 1965, p. 238). Of course, to anyone familiar with

Tanaka's globalist jurisprudence over the previous decades, it would come as no surprise that he would elevate the basic principle of international law, *pacta sunt servanda* ("treaties must be observed") over municipal law, including the Constitution. No doubt, Tanaka's long commitment to World Law influenced his understanding of the priority of international treaties and his tendency to avoid positivist interpretations of the Constitution in favor a globalist one.[6]

In 1960, Tanaka would reach the mandatory retirement age of seventy on his birthday, October 24. In 1961, he reflected that he had hoped to retire from public service to a quiet life of reading and reflection (Tanaka 1961, p. 88). That may be so, but it is also true that in March 1960 he had announced his candidacy for the open position on the International Court of Justice (ICJ) in The Hague, and he had spent much of August and September that year traveling through America, Argentina, Austria, France, Portugal, Spain, and Tunisia, meeting leading jurists and political leaders as part of his campaign for the position. After his return to Japan, Tanaka was awarded the Order of Culture on November 3 by the Emperor in recognition of his many contributions to commercial law and world law. And less than a month after his retirement, he was elected by the United Nations to a nine-year term on the ICJ. He described the move in colorful and self-effacing terms: "No sooner had I been released from the ivory tower of the Supreme Court, than I had to spend the next nine years on the other side of the world living like an exile in a hotel in The Hague in the Netherlands" (Tanaka 1961, p. 88). He credited his election to the ICJ to efforts by Japan's diplomatic corps, beginning with Foreign Minister Kosaka Zentarō, and particularly to his life-long sponsor, the ninety year old Professor Yamada Saburō. But he did not neglect the fact that he was helped by the many friends he had made in his travels to France, Italy and Latin America over the past decades (Tanaka 1961, pp. 88–89). Tanaka's unyielding commitment to globalism in law and culture had paid off: he was now recognized as one of the leading global jurists in the world.

Tanaka sat on the ICJ from February 1961 to February 1970. The Court heard nine cases during his term, although he only participated in eight of them. Excluding jurisdiction hearings and a budget request, there were only five substantive cases: the Temple of Preah Vihear Case of 1961–1962, the South West Africa Case of 1962–1966, the Northern Cameroons Case of 1963, the Barcelona Traction, Light and Power Company Case of 1964–1970, and the North Sea Continental

Shelf Case of 1969. Following Takano Yūichi's lead (Takano 1977, pp. 198–220), I will focus on three cases (the Barcelona Traction Case, the North Sea Continental Shelf Case and the South West Africa Case) where Tanaka either submitted a separate opinion or a dissenting opinion as such circumstances offer the best insight into his own jurisprudence. In the Barcelona Traction Case, Belgium filed suit against Spain, arguing that Spain was responsible for violations of international law that caused injury to a Canadian corporation (the Barcelona Traction, Light and Power Company) and its Belgian shareholders that was operating in Spanish territory. The ICJ found that Belgium lacked legal standing and therefore rejected the Belgium government's claim by a vote of 15 to 1. Tanaka agreed that Belgium's complaint of injustice was unfounded but he felt the reasoning of the ICJ was erroneous. Instead of the theory of institutional "lapse" between the prewar Permanent Court of Justice and the ICJ, Tanaka argued for "sociological and teleological approaches" that were essential to the field of international law. He was, as he had throughout his career, arguing for the primacy of the ideals of justice and peace over institutionalism and legal positivism (*International Court of Justice*, "Separate Opinion of Judge Tanaka," p. 75).

The North Sea Continental Shelf Case comprised a series of disputes between Germany, Denmark and the Netherlands regarding the delimitation of parts of the continental shelf in the North Sea. Denmark and the Netherlands wanted to apply the equidistance rule that would have given Germany a smaller portion than its preferred method of measure based on coastline length. The Court was asked to decide whether either customary law or the Geneva Convention had determined that States were obligated to accept the equidistance principle of delimitation. The Court decided that equidistance was not an obligatory method for delimitation. In his dissenting opinion, Tanaka stressed that, in contrast to positivists and voluntarists, "those who advocate the objective existence of law apart from the will of States, are inclined to take a more liberal and elastic attitude in recognizing the formation of a customary law attributing more importance to the evaluation of the content of law than to the process of its formation" (*International Court of Justice*, "Dissenting Opinion of Judge Tanaka," Continental Shelf Case, p. 178). He left no doubt that he belonged in the latter group. Perhaps the most surprising argument Tanaka made was to reject the Federal Republic of Germany's appeal to the Natural Law. He noted that "natural law does not venture to interfere with positive law except in the case that positive law rules are manifestly immoral and violate the principles of natural law. Such a case cannot occur in the matter of the equidistance principle" (*International Court of Justice*, "Dissenting Opinion of Judge Tanaka, Continental Shelf Case," p. 193). On the contrary, he found sufficient historical grounds to consider the equidistance principle as legitimate and ended by regretting that the ICJ missed an opportunity to accord "the equidistance principle the status of a world law ... [and thus] make a contribution to the progressive development of international law" (*International Court of Justice*, "Dissenting Opinion of Judge Tanaka, Continental Shelf Case," p. 197).

Of the three cases, clearly the South West Africa Case was the most significant. And it provided a counter-example to the North Sea Continental Shelf Case insofar as Tanaka found it a highly appropriate context for the application of Natural Law over against positive law. South West Africa (today, Namibia) was a colony of Germany that after World War I became a mandate of the Union of South Africa. After World War II, South Africa refused to turn it over to the United Nations, as required, and continued to rule the territory, bringing it under its apartheid system. On November 4, 1960 Ethiopia and Liberia, as former States Member of the League of Nations, filed separate claims against South Africa in the ICJ, challenging South African rule over the territory. The following year, the ICJ combined the two cases into one. After challenges from South Africa to the ICJ's jurisdiction failed, the court ruled on the matter on July 18, 1966. The ICJ was evenly split 7-7, so the vote of the President Sir Percy Spender determined the judgment in South Africa's favor, rejecting the claim that Ethiopia and Liberia had a legal interest in the case. Had circumstances not led to a number of judges being disqualified or absent, the vote probably would have been 10-7 against South Africa (Tonchi et al. 2012, p. 180).

Tanaka's seventy-four page, nuanced dissenting opinion was such a model of international jurisprudence that it is still cited today in law journals. It was also a beautiful summary of his legal thinking over a career that had encompassed much of the twentieth century. In the 1930s, he had outlined a theory of World Law precisely to respond to the narrow, positivist bias in international law that was limited to relations among States and their respective interests. He returned to the basic principles of that theory of World Law in his dissent, arguing that

> each member of a human society—whether domestic or international—is interested in the realization of social justice and humanitarian ideas. The State which belongs as a member to an international organization incorporating such ideas must necessarily be interested. So far as the interest in this case affects the rights and obligations of a State, it may be called a legal interest. The State may become the subject or holder of a legal interest regarding social justice and humanitarian matters, but this interest includes its profound concern with the attitude of other States, particularly member States belonging to the same treaty or organization. In short, each State may possess a legal interest in the observance of the obligations by other States. (*International Court of Justice*, "Dissenting Opinion of Judge Tanaka," South West Africa Case, p. 253)

In applying the principles of World Law to the South West Africa Case, Tanaka noted that a key difference between international law and World Law was that international law was inter-State in nature, whereas World Law speaks to fundamental human rights that transcend the rights and responsibilities established through treaties and other positive laws. Was a State responsible for the protection of human rights in the international arena, as it is within its own territory? Tanaka held that it was, since "the existence of human rights does not depend on the will of a State; neither internally on its law or any other legislative measure, nor internationally on treaty or custom, in which the express or tacit will of a State constitutes the essential element" (*International Court of Justice*, "Dissenting Opinion of Judge Tanaka," South West Africa Case, p. 297). Human rights are upheld by the Natural Law, and thus they exist whether a State recognizes them or not, and they exist even where State authority does not extend.

At first glance, Tanaka would seem to be contradicting himself in applying the Natural Law to the South West Africa Case, yet rejecting the Federal Republic of Germany's assertion of the Natural Law in its defense in the North Sea Continental Shelf Case. We have seen that in the North Sea Continental Case, Tanaka pointed out that the technical choice of a method of measurement is not of the nature of a fundamental human right, and thus he rejected the appeal to the Natural Law in that context. But in the South West Africa Case, the issue was really whether racial discrimination was consistent with the rule of law. Tanaka held that it was not, because it directly violated a key principle of law:

> The most fundamental point in the equality principle is that all human beings as persons have an equal value in themselves, that they are the aim itself and not means for others, and that, therefore, slavery is denied. The idea of equality of men as persons and equal treatment as such is of a metaphysical nature. It underlies all modern, democratic and humanitarian law systems as a principle of natural law … . Consequently, the practice of apartheid is fundamentally unreason-able and unjust. The unreasonableness and injustice do not depend upon the intention or motive of the Mandatory, namely its *mala fides*. Distinction on a racial basis is in itself contrary to the principle of equality which is of the character of natural law, and accordingly illegal. (*International Court of Justice*, "Dissenting Opinion of Judge Tanaka," South West Africa Case, pp. 305–314)

Tanaka may have lost the battle, but he won the war. On October 27, just three months after Tanaka lost the vote on the South West Africa Case, the General Assembly of the United Nations passed Resolution 2145 that declared that the Republic of South Africa had no further right to administer South West Africa. In 1971, acting on a request for an Advisory Opinion from the United Nations Security Council, the ICJ ruled that the continued presence of South Africa in Namibia was illegal and that South Africa was under an obligation to withdraw from Namibia immediately. It did not, so war between Namibia and South Africa continued, until 1989. But the trends in world opinion—and eventually the world court—definitely supported Tanaka's 1966 dissent, as did the ultimate resolution of the conflict. Surely Tanaka was disappointed that the situation was not resolved at the level of the world court until after he had stepped down and—had he lived long enough to see it—that the ultimate resolution came through violence rather than through the law. Still, he was a seasoned jurist who knew quite well that defending basic principles of justice was more important than winning every case. And he had won his share, both as Chief Justice of the Japanese Supreme Court and as a judge for nearly a decade on the ICJ.

Tanaka was the first Japanese judge on the ICJ, but he was not the first Japanese to sit on a world court. In a book dedicated to Judge Oda Shigeru, Tanaka's successor on the ICJ, Kinji Akashi compares and contrasts Tanaka with Japan's first globally recognized jurists: Oda Yorozu, Adachi Mineichirō and Nagaoka Harukazu who sat on the Permanent Court of International Justice (PCJ) at various times between 1921 and 1942. Akashi points out that, in contrast to his predecessors on the PCJ, Tanaka, with his strong background in jurisprudence,

> was aware of methodology in international law. With this knowledge, and through the experience of World War II and the militarist régime in Japan, he realized the defects in relying simply on the positivistic method and positive norms of international law that had been constructed by the Westerners. He thus challenged the then prevailing but from his viewpoint, insufficient positive norms by introducing natural law. His argument was a challenge to the Western-made system of international law by means of Western-made method … . After the age of the good followers with passive attitudes, the active attitude displayed by Tanaka indicated the commencement of the active Japanese contribution to the development of the jurisprudence of international law. (Akashi 2002, pp. 21–22)

After Tanaka and Oda, two other Japanese have also sat on the ICJ: the father of Crown Princess Masako, Owada Hisashi (2002–2018) and Iwasawa Yūji (2018–present). While all of the Japanese who have sat on a world court are distinguished jurists, it may be said that none was as committed to the principles and practice of World Law as Tanaka. His achievement in defending globalist principles in law and culture was recognized at the end of his judicial career in two ways. In February 1970, just as he retired from the ICJ, Tanaka was appointed an Honorary Councilor to the Vatican. And on April 29, he was awarded the Grand Cordon of the Order of the Paulownia Flowers by the Emperor of Japan. Nothing better expresses Tanaka's globalism, a globalism that incorporated his cultural particularity as a Japanese, than these two nearly simultaneous awards: one that recognized his extraordinary contributions to the Japanese nation and the other that demonstrated the exceptional trust and respect accorded him by the universal Catholic Church.

Notes

1. Tanaka himself gives credit to Mibuchi's wife's influence, but also notes that he gave Mibuchi many books on Catholicism to read. Tanaka was Mibuchi's godfather. See Sano (2009, pp. 2–3).
2. Tanaka calls Carpenter the Chief of Legal Affairs Section in 1950, as do other histories of the time period. He appears to have been brought back in to substitute for Oppler at this time, as he is not listed as an employee of Government Section in the cumulative listing of those working for G-S between 1945 and 1948. See Supreme Commander for the Allied Powers, Government Section (1948, pp. 811, 816).
3. Cf. Tanaka (1954c, 1955a, b, 1958b). Most were reprinted in various other works, and all were included in *Tanaka Kōtarō chosakushū*, volume 5.

4. A "perfect crime" (*kanzen hanzai*) is a crime that is never detected by the authorities. In the aftermath of the suspicious and unsolved death of Shimoyama, this was a particularly serious threat against Tanaka.
5. Although this case is more commonly referred to as the "Sunagawa Case" in recent media accounts, I use the term "Sunakawa Case" in keeping with the terminology of the official English records of the Supreme Court and English language newspaper reports of the time.
6. Makihara Izuru presents a different but compatible theory that focuses on domestic issues rather than global ones. To Makihara, Tanaka's decision in the Sunakawa Case, along with other of his decisions in the Supreme Court, reflects his "partial society" (*bubun shakai*) theory that, rejecting social totalitarianism, respected "diversity in the legal order" (*hō chitsujo no tagensei*). "Partial society" refers to a complex sociological theory that essentially says Tanaka respected the different functions of the legislature and the courts. See Makihara (2012, pp. 224–230).

References

Akashi, Kinji. 2002. Japanese Predecessors of Judge Shigeru Oda in the World Courts: Works and Method. In *Liber Amicorum: Judge Shigeru Oda*, vol. 1, ed. Nisuke Ando, Edward McWhinney, and Rüdiger Wolfrum. The Hague, London and New York: Kluwer Law International.

Asahi Shimbun. 1950a. Isasaka ginen. Wednesday, March 1, p. 1.

———. 1950b. Shasetsu: Saikōsai shin-chōkan ni nozomu. Wednesday, March 1, p. 1.

International Court of Justice. Separate Opinion of Judge Tanaka. http://www.icj-cij.org/files/case-related/50/050-19700205-JUD-01-05-EN.pdf. Accessed 31 July 2018.

———. Dissenting Opinion of Judge Tanaka, Continental Shelf Case. http://www.icj-cij.org/files/case-related/52/052-19690220-JUD-01-08-EN.pdf. Accessed 31 July 2018.

———. Dissenting Opinion of Judge Tanaka, South West Africa Case. http://www.icj-cij.org/files/case-related/47/047-19660718-JUD-01-06-EN.pdf. Accessed 31 July 2018.

Makihara, Izuru. 2012. 'Bubun shakai' to 'zōge no tō': Mibuchi Tadahiko to Tanaka Kōtarō. In *Seiji o ikiru: rekishi to gendai no tōshizu*, ed. Iio Jun, Karube Tadashi, and Makihara Izuru. Chūō Kōron Shinsha: Tokyo.

Nippon Times. 1950a. The New Chief Justice. Wednesday, March 1, p. 2.

———. 1950b. Mibuchi Becomes Catholic. Saturday, March 4, p. 3.

———. 1956. Chief Justice Going Abroad. Sunday, January 8, p. 1.

Sakata *v.* Japan (The Sunakawa Case), trans. Charles R. Steven and Kazunobu Takahashi. In *Japanese Law in Context: Readings in Society, the Economy, and*

Politics, ed. Curtis J. Milhaupt, J. Mark Ramseyer, and Michael K. Young. Cambridge, MA and London: Harvard University Asia Center, 2001.

Sano, Hiromi. 2009. Kyōzai 'Roku o sabaku' kō (3). *Kushiro ronshū: hokkaidō kyōiku daigaku kushiro kō kenkyū kiyō, number* 41: 1–11.

Sekiguchi, Tai. 1950. Shin chōkan o kataru. *Asahi Shimbun*. Wednesday, March 1, p. 1.

Supreme Commander for the Allied Powers, Government Section. 1948. *Political Reorientation of Japan, September 1945 to September 1948*. Washington, DC: U.S. Government Printing Office.

Supreme Court of Japan. 1957. Decision in the Lady Chatterly's Lover Case. http://www.courts.go.jp/app/files/hanrei_jp/271/051271_hanrei.pdf. Accessed 30 July 2018.

———. 1959. Judgment upon Case of the So-Called "SUNAKAWA CASE". http://www.courts.go.jp/app/hanrei_en/detail?id=13. Accessed 30 July 2018.

Takano, Yūichi. 1977. Kokusai shihō saibansho to Tanaka Kōtarō hakase. In *Tanaka Kōtarō: hito to gyōseki*, ed. Suzuki Takeo. Tokyo: Yūhikaku.

Tanaka, Kōtarō. 1950. Address by Dr. Paul Francis Kotaro Tanaka on the Occasion of Conferring Honorary Degree of Doctor of Laws by the [sic] Georgetown University. October 29. Tanaka Kōtarō Archives (13) 4, Department of Law, Tokyo University.

———. 1952. Peace and Justice: Japan's Place in the Family of Nations. *American Bar Association Journal* 38 (August): 663–675.

———. 1953a. *Amerika kikō*. Tokyo: Yomiuri Shimbun Sha.

———. 1953b. The Democratization of the Japanese Administration of Justice. In *Japan's Problems*. Tokyo: Ministry of Foreign Affairs, Public Information and Cultural Affairs. The copy of this publication that I possess is an offprint, paged 1 through 14.

———. 1954a. Hō to sekai. In *Heiwa no hō tetsugaku*. Tokyo: Yūhikaku; reprinted in Tanaka 1972.

———. 1954b. In Defense of the Supreme Court. *Nippon Times*, Monday, June 14, p. 8.

———. 1954c. Saibankan no ryōshin to dokuritsu ni tsuite. *Hōsō Jihō* 7 (1) (December 15); reprinted in *Tanaka Kōtarō chosakushū* volume 5: pp. 559–590. Tokyo Shunjū Sha, 1964.

———. 1955a. Saiban to yoron. *Jurisuto* (August 1); reprinted in *Tanaka Kōtarō chosakushū* volume 5: pp. 373–406. Tokyo Shunjū Sha, 1964.

———. 1955b. "Saiban." *Hō tetsugaku kōza, volume 8: Hō no shihai to saiban*. Tokyo: Yūhikaku; reprinted in *Tanaka Kōtarō chosakushū* volume 5: pp. 347–372. Tokyo Shunjū Sha, 1964.

———. 1958a. *Burajiru kara mekishiko e*. Tokyo: Shunjū Sha.

———. 1958b. Saiban to hōdō no jiyū. *Jurisuto* (January 1); reprinted in *Tanaka Kōtarō chosakushū* volume 5: pp. 439–468. Tokyo Shunjū Sha, 1964.

———. 1961. *Watakushi no rirekisho*. Tokyo: Shunjū Sha.
———. 1965. Japanese Law. In *Sovereignty Within the Law*, ed. Arthur Larson and C. Wilfred Jenks, et al. Dobbs Ferry, NY: Oceana Publications.
Tonchi, Victor L., William A. Lindeke, John J. Grotpeter. 2012. *Historical Dictionary of Namibia*. Lanham: Scarecrow Press.
Wikipedia-Japan. Mibuchi Tadahiko. https://ja.wikipedia.org/wiki/三淵忠彦. Accessed 24 July 2018.
Yomiuri Shimbun. 1950. Oshiruko to kenpō no bannin: Tanaka-san nichiyōbi no 'tsurushiage'. Monday, March 6, p. 2.
———. 1958. Saikōsai e tōsho senjutsu: kyōhakubun nado sanzen yo tsū. October 5, p. 11.
———. 1959. Kensei ya engekika: 'zatsuon' ni madowasareru na. May 25, p. 5.

CHAPTER 6

Tanaka's Final Years—And Beyond

Abstract This short concluding chapter covers Tanaka's final publications from 1970 until his death in 1974. A key point is that two of his major articles during these final years were published in English, reaching a global readership. The chapter then assesses his legacy today, concluding that his globalist jurisprudence, his defense of the Natural Law, and even his Catholic faith—the font of his globalist values—deserve renewed attention particularly since, as a respected Japanese scholar and jurist, Tanaka resists any easy reduction of this globalism to mere expressions of Western culture.

Keywords World Law · International Court of Justice · Zagreb Human rights · Peace and Justice · Natural Law

In February 1970, Tanaka's term on the International Court of Justice (ICJ) expired and he returned to Japan. Retirement was not an easy adjustment for Tanaka. He reflected that if the university was his first home, the courts had become his second home (Tanaka 1961, p. 88). And with reason. He had spent about the same amount of time, roughly twenty years, in each institution. Those close to Tanaka believed that his years on the ICJ had taken a heavy toll on his health and may even have shortened his life.[1] He never regained his usual energy after returning to Japan and in fact spent much of the next four years checking in and out

K. M. Doak, *Tanaka Kōtarō and World Law*, Global Political Thinkers,
https://doi.org/10.1007/978-3-030-02035-4_6

of the nearby International Catholic Hospital (*Seibo Byōin*) for treatment of various illnesses.

And yet, even as a weakened octogenarian, Tanaka continued to make contributions to global thought, regularly publishing articles in journals and newspapers. Within a few months of returning to Japan, he penned "Civilization and Morality" and published it in the journal *Kokoro*. In it, he returned to a key point from his 1946 lecture to the Emperor which we saw above in Chapter 4—how the Japanese had only incorporated material civilization from the West while leaving aside spiritual civilization. His point now was not limited to the Emperor; it was that all of Japanese society needed to realize that no law or institution can serve the people if the people's morality is weak. And he emphasized a key theme from his tenure in the Ministry of Education—that education should be about the "perfection of the person" (*jinkaku no kansei*), not mere utilitarian skills to train future employees. In contrast to the West, he found Japan to be not merely a country of natural disasters, but a country of man-made disasters that stemmed from a generally weak sense of moral responsibility among the people. His evidence ranged from frequent house fires, gas explosions caused by workmen's negligence, traffic accidents and even the "word pollution" (*moji ni yotte sōon*) of the ubiquitous and pointless slogans plastered on community notice boards, to food manufacturers who put toxic preservatives in their products and corporate executives whose lack of social responsibility had caused great damage to the nation. Rather than seeing these problems as generic to modern society, Tanaka located their causes in Japanese society at a particular moment in time:

> The spread of the ideologies of positivism and historical materialism in our country after the First World War gave priority to political and economic values and subordinated law and morality under them as methods. We Japanese must be clear about the proper order among various values and recover the authority of morality. A correct interpretation of the Fundamental Law of Education requires this more than anything else. (Tanaka 1970, p. 7)

The proper order of values for Tanaka was one that put man first and material things second. Even in economic transactions, the basis was relations of trust among people (a point he had made decades earlier in his *Theory of World Law*). He was still a globalist who believed that the

Japanese could and should learn from other countries. He cited Rudolph Stammler's argument that law is not superstructure to an economic base but is in fact the base of the economic order since it is about regulating human relationships. Or, in Tanaka's own words, "anything man-made has a human element breathed into it," and thus cannot be separated from morality (Tanaka 1970, p. 9).

Perhaps the most globalist of Tanaka's later articles was his 1971 English language article on "The Character of World Law in the International Court of Justice" (with a Japanese translation appearing the following year.) In it, Tanaka drew from his personal experience on the court to argue that the ICJ increasingly was becoming an embodiment of the principles of World Law that he had outlined forty years earlier. First, he pointed to the composition of the court, noting that a judge on the ICJ "is elected on the basis of his personal qualification. He neither represents a State nor a certain form of civilization or legal system. In this sense, the composition of the Court is not international but global" (Tanaka 1971a, pp. 14–15). We saw above in Chapter 3 how Tanaka had built his concept of World Law on a repudiation of the realist theory of international law that was based on the sovereignty of the State. Now, he could demonstrate the reality of World Law through his personal experience of how the ICJ was structured, governed and functioned. In the first place, the ICJ had adopted many of the procedures of the Permanent Court of International Justice (PCJ), even though institutionally that court, along with the League of Nations, had ceased to exist. This was a refutation of the positivists and international jurists who held that law was only found in statutes or treaties that political institutions like States had created. The trans-institutional reality that linked the PCJ with the ICJ revealed a non-institutional continuity that classic international jurisprudence could not explain. Tanaka could. He pointed out that with the adoption of the Resolution Concerning the International Judicial Practice of the ICJ in 1968 which had "no connection to any specific legal system or the institutions of any particular State. … the International Court of Justice has taken on a world law rather than an international aspect in its personnel structure and its procedural practices" (Tanaka 1971a, pp. 18–19). Hence, he concluded that the general public was not mistaken in referring to the ICJ informally as "the World Court," as it was in fact based on World Law (Tanaka 1971a, p. 11).

In addition to its composition and governing principles, the ICJ was a manifestation of the reality of World Law in terms of the type of law that it applied in its cases. According to the Statute of the ICJ, the court is to apply three sources of law in its decisions: "(a) international conventions …; (b) international custom …; [and] (c) the general principles of law recognized by civilized nations."[2] Tanaka admitted that (a) and (b) do not escape the scope of positivist jurisprudence, as States determine conventions and what constitutes custom in their locale. But he pointed out that the third category, "the general principles of law," alone "binds States regardless of their will" (Tanaka 1971a, p. 19). And he argued that this third category of law was not inferior to the other two but in fact "logically speaking, the general principles of law precede rather than follow conventions and international custom. Thus the general principles of law are the universal principles—so-called judicial truth or natural law" (Tanaka 1971a, p. 21).[3]

Since Tanaka was not a positivist, he would not be satisfied with statutes and the like as conclusive evidence for the ICJ as an instantiation of World Law. He had long argued that law originates in society (*ubi societas ibi ius*) and that for World Law to exist there must also exist a world society, or "world community" (see Chapter 5). That is where his argument seemed to falter. He himself had conceded in his 1952 "Peace and Justice" article that the Cold War world was not one unified community but in fact was divided into two: the Free World and the Communist World. Nor did he retract that argument in the early 1970s. The key question for the existence of a World Court (and of course for World Law) was "whether liberalistic States can peacefully co-exist with communist States under an international rule of law" (Tanaka 1971a, p. 16). If communist States were true to their historical materialism and maintained that law was merely a superstructure, a means to be used for political objectives, then there was little ground for an affirmative answer to the key question. However, Tanaka pointed out that the communist bloc did not appear to be treating law in the manner historical materialism mandated, at least at the level of international policy. Moreover, he referred to the fact that relations between communist States and liberal States had grown closer over time—even if those relations were not always amicable. Consequently, he concluded that

> the communist States must acknowledge that a relationship of social interdependence actually exists between themselves and the capitalist States.

> Furthermore, acknowledgment of a social relationship implies, to a certain extent, the recognition of the existence of legal norms. *Ubi societas ibi ius.* As long as an economic or any other kind of relationship prevails at all, the basis for such a relationship ought to be, at the very least, the norm of *pacta sunt servanda.* Even where no treaty or other form of positive law has been established between the States, no one can deny the presence of the rule of natural law. (Tanaka 1971a, p. 17)

Finally, he pointed out that the challenges of a common legal community in the international world with communist and liberal blocs was not substantially different from the challenges faced domestically in countries like Japan that have legally recognized communist parties and liberal parties. Whether between States in the world community or among judges on the ICJ, "legal heterogeneity … is not so great as their political heterogeneity" (Tanaka 1971a, p. 17). In conclusion, Tanaka found that, even with the divisions in the international community during the Cold War, there was still a world community and thus, on that basis, there must exist also a World Law.

Once again, Tanaka put his ideas into practice. In late August 1971, he attended the general meeting of the Institute of International Law in Zagreb, the capital of the Socialist Republic of Croatia, one of the republics in the Socialist Federal Republic of Yugoslavia under the dictatorship of Josip Borz Tito. Croatia was a perfect test case for his theory of a common legal understanding within and across the political heterogeneity of the world order. Formally a Communist State but distanced from the Soviet Union after 1948, Croatia was also an overwhelmingly Catholic nation and Zagreb itself was the historic center of Croatian nationalism. In an article called "Zagreb" that he published shortly after his return to Japan, Tanaka confessed that he had not been able to conduct much research on Croatian history and culture before leaving for the conference, and in fact he had fallen ill with acute pyelitis immediately after the meeting and had to spend the ten days he had hoped to use for personal excursions instead convalescing in his hotel room in Dubrovnik. But he did reflect that in Zagreb Sunday Masses were quite packed both at St. Mark's Church and at the Cathedral of the Assumption of Mary, and he recognized that Zagreb was a "rival" to the capital of Yugoslavia, Belgrade (Tanaka 1971b, p. 390). Such laconic remarks as these suggest that either Tanaka knew a good deal more about Croatia than he admitted, or that his sharp instincts and powers of observation served him well in quickly grasping the cultural and political diversity in Yugoslavia.

Tanaka's last major article was published in English. "Some Observations on Peace, Law, and Human Rights" first appeared as a chapter in a 1972 volume published in honor of Philip C. Jessup, Tanaka's colleague on the ICJ (the chapter was also published in Japanese the following year in Tanaka's *Sequel to A Theory of World Law*). It was a fitting conclusion to Tanaka's long life as a globalist intellectual. It was less institutional in focus than his previous article on the ICJ, but no less a defense of World Law, universal human rights, and the moral obligation to intervene when necessary in the internal affairs of a State to protect human rights. Firstly, Tanaka re-stated the fact that highly developed networks of social and economic intercourse had demonstrated "the existence of a world community in which world law is not only a *Sollen* but a *Sein*" and that this was a "world law that imposes limitations upon the sovereignty of each state" (Tanaka 1972, p. 243). Secondly, he emphasized the relationship of international peace with what he called its *condition sine qua non*, the rule of World Law. And thirdly, he argued that since human rights were an inherent part of justice, true world peace could not be achieved without a universal "agreement on the desirability and degree of protection of human rights and fundamental freedoms" (Tanaka 1972, p. 247). He conceded that at present such an agreement was lacking in terms of positive law and strong enforcement mechanisms. But he did not concede that therefore human rights had to be denied as a legal reality. Tanaka's conclusion was that

> the lack of definition of 'human rights and fundamental freedoms' in the Charter [of the United Nations] and in later legislation and the absence of juridical mechanisms for enforcing them do not constitute a reason for denying their existence or the need for their legal protection. That a norm is *lex imperfecta* does not deprive it of its legal character. (Tanaka 1972, p. 250)

Tanaka firmly believed that World Law was a necessary conclusion to the legal questions that had been raised by the Second World War, particularly by the atrocities committed by Nazi Germany and Imperial Japan. Those war crimes had shocked the moral conscience of the world but some still defended them on traditional positivist legal grounds, particularly the principle of *nulla poena sine lege* ("no penalty without a law").

As a globalist jurist, Tanaka realized that international law had to be dislodged from its positivist bias and reconstructed on a new foundation in World Law in order to respond effectively to the legal and moral challenges those war crimes had left in their wake.

But the challenges to the dignity of the human person were not limited to crimes committed by States during war. Tanaka's experience during the postwar period had also shown him the dangers to human rights that came from one's fellow citizens, especially when moral relativism and liberalism had created a culture in which each man was his own moral authority and truth was deemed subjective, at best. Tanaka's rebuttal to individualistic moral relativism was direct: "if an individual had authority to determine what is good and right, what is bad and unjust, he would be 'the measure of all things' (Protagoras) and the creator of truth, usurping the position of God. On that hypothesis any abuse of freedoms and rights could be justified" (Tanaka 1972, p. 250). Tanaka returned to his earlier distinction, developed in his study of negotiable instruments (see Chapter 2) between those laws that are reflective of local customs and religions and those laws that are universally valid. The protection of universal human rights was, of course, not of a technical legal nature (as many universal laws were), but one of a profoundly moral nature. As he had throughout his career, Tanaka found the basis for this morality which was not limited to particular cultures or religions in the Natural Law, which itself is rooted in human nature. The alternative was to think that human rights only exist to the extent a State or international organization had codified them in its positive laws—and if so, then such institutions could also negate human rights by changing their legal codes. In addition, Tanaka recognized that while the principle of human rights is clear, the enumeration of specific human rights is less so. Legal codification of human rights cannot be considered either an absolute limitation on fundamental human rights nor a condition of their existence. Tanaka's conclusion to "Some Observations on Peace, Law, and Human Rights" sums up his argument succinctly and eloquently, and indeed may be taken as the last public words of this remarkable, globalist intellectual:

> Human rights comprise many different rights that are still imperfectly developed. They include the right to life, liberty, and security of person; freedom from arbitrary arrest and detention; the right to a fair trial; freedom of thought, conscience, religion and expression; freedom of peaceful

> assembly and association; the right to equal protection of the law. These and other rights and freedoms are *conditiones sine qua non* of a democratic society, required for the purpose of attaining the end of life, which is the participation of the human being in the historical process of creation. They emanate from the status of man as "person." They are an indivisible, integral whole, one status and no more. The protection and guarantee of human rights are a minimum requirement and a common denominator of democratic communities, giving those communities a political homogeneity which is one of the essential conditions of world peace. (Tanaka 1972, pp. 255–256)

In a fitting gesture of respect for this aging Japanese globalist, the Vatican reappointed him as an Honorary Councilor in May 1973.

Tanaka was already seriously ill. He was readmitted to the International Catholic Hospital that summer, complaining he had no appetite for food or drink. He was released from the hospital briefly, but readmitted after complaints that his appetite still had not returned and he had inexplicable pain in his hips. Released, he was readmitted again on February 14, 1974 for treatment of bronchitis; this time, he never left the hospital. One of the last people to talk with Tanaka was Sister Takamine Sadako who worked in the hospital and often stopped by his room. One day, shortly before he died, he suddenly told her that he found hospital life hard. When Sister Sadako asked him whether he meant he was in some kind of pain, physical or spiritual, he told her that "the hard part is having all your desires indulged" (Takamine 1974, p. 461). Tanaka Kōtarō died of cardiac malfunction on March 1, 1974 and a Mass of Christian Burial was held for him at the Tokyo Cathedral at 11:00 a.m. on Monday, March 4. He was posthumously awarded the Grand Cordon of the Supreme Order of the Chrysanthemum, only the fifth person to receive this honor in the postwar period and the sole awardee who had not served as prime minister.

How to sum up the many contributions Tanaka Kōtarō made to globalism over the course of his long life? We should begin by recognizing a few unusual facts about him. First, he was the only Japanese in modern history to serve in all three branches of the government. He was the longest serving Chief Justice of the Japanese Supreme Court and during his tenure he played a key role in establishing the independence of the Court. He was the first Japanese to serve on the International Court of Justice. He also was one of the few, if not the only, Japanese to be able to accept the prewar Meiji Constitution and to embrace the postwar Constitution of Japan without undergoing a radical conversion (*tenkō*) in his thinking. He could do so because he was not a positivist but understood all positive laws as imperfect efforts to reach the perfection of the Natural Law. By the same token, it is unlikely that he would have resisted all efforts to revise the current Constitution of Japan to make it more effective in protecting human rights, as national and international circumstances changed. Tanaka's legal pragmatism held that all laws can be improved on, and his moral idealism held that it was incumbent on us to do so when necessary and possible. His consistent, principled thought was also applied in criticizing anyone who would use violence against basic human rights, whether they were on the political right or the political left. He opposed the violence of the rightwing militarists and communists in prewar Japan and, after the demise of militarism in postwar Japan, maintained his opposition to communism at home and abroad. He was a globalist in Imperial Japan, frequently travelling around the world (especially to Europe and Latin America), and again in postwar Japan when he expanded his globalism to include not only America but India, the Dominican Republic and other countries. Another measure of his globalism is the number of awards he received from countries around the world: the Magna Cruce Equitem Ordinis Sancti Silvestro Papa from the Vatican (1953), the Orden del Marito de Duart, Sanchez y Mella: Gran Cruz Placa de Plata from the Dominican Republic (1956), the Grâ-Cruz da Ordem Nacional do Crúzeiro do Sul from Brazil (1957), the Grand Cordon de l'Ordre Tharge from Iran (1958), the Medaglia d'Oro per i Benemeriti della Cultura Italiana from Italy (1958), the Gross Kreuz des Verdienstordens from the Federal Republic of Germany (1960), and he was made a Grand Officier Légion d'honneur by France (1960); he received honorary doctorates from Boston College, Fordham University, and Georgetown University in the United States and from the Catholic University of Chile; in addition, he received a total of four decorations from the Emperor of Japan.

Of course, these measures of Tanaka's international recognition do not get to the heart of his intellectual contributions to globalism. A better measure might be how his ideas have or have not circulated in the intellectual world since his death. Not surprisingly, there has been far greater attention to Tanaka's thought in Japanese scholarship than in other languages. In the late 1980s and early 1990s, important Japanese intellectual historians like Mitani Ta'ichirō and Hanzawa Takamaro drew considerable attention to Tanaka, especially his theory of the Natural Law. A considerable boost to the study of Tanaka's thought in Japanese was the reprinting of his ten volume *Collected Works* in 1998 by Shinsei Publishers. In its selection from Tanaka's voluminous publications, the *Collected Works* emphasized Tanaka's writings on commercial law and other technical legal studies (although not completely excluding some of his key works on social and moral thought). So perhaps it is not surprising that beginning in the early 2000s with Uemura Tatsuo of Waseda University and down to 2016 with Eiji Takahashi of Osaka City University, law professors in Japan have focused on contributions made by Tanaka's early studies in corporate governance, while leaving aside his later, more philosophical work.[4] This interest in Tanaka's legal work has of course been represented in English, especially by scholars who draw on his later work in human rights and World Law, given the availability in English of his opinions on the ICJ.[5] Most recently, Keisuke Takeshita has published an important analysis of Tanaka's World Law in English as part of his broader reassessment of the significance of universal private international law.[6] Outside of more technical legal studies, there are approaches like that of Koga Katsujirō who builds on Tanaka's studies in Chinese Confucianism and Legalism to link Mozi's concept of *ken'ai* with Christian understandings of *caritas* as part of a broader argument for the universal norm of rule of law under a nation-state (Koga 2014, pp. 320–321). Others in Japan have focused on Tanaka's contribution to education, especially in drafting the Fundamental Law on Education.[7] And Shibasaki Atsushi has written several articles in recent years (in English and Japanese) as well as a major book chapter on aspects of Tanaka's thought related to global cultural relations (see for example, Shibasaki 2010). Unfortunately, there has been less attention to Tanaka as an intellectual in the English language scholarship, particularly in recent decades. This book is a step towards bringing Tanaka back to his rightful place as one of the twentieth century's leading globalist intellectuals.

Tanaka Kōtarō claims our attention as an important globalist intellectual in large part because of his original jurisprudence, particularly his theory of World Law. In developing a substantial theory of World Law as distinct from international law, Tanaka offers a major contribution to globalist thinking. At the same time, by placing his conception of World Law on solid footing in the Natural Law, Tanaka presents a strong counter-argument to those who maintain that the Natural Law is nothing more than a particular cultural artifact of Western civilization, or even of medieval European culture. As a modern, Japanese jurist who embraced the Natural Law as a globally valid means of understanding universal truth, Tanaka stands as a powerful challenge to cultural and philosophical relativists. A similar thing can and should be said about Tanaka's acceptance of the Catholic faith, which came about not from the preaching of any Western missionary but by his own intellectual search for that which is universally true. Cultural and philosophical relativism remain today as among the greatest obstacles to globalism. In such a time of intellectual confusion and cultural retreat into regionalism and nationalism, Tanaka Kōtarō reminds us of the better angels of our common human nature.

Notes

1. See comments by Tanaka Jirō, Toyosaki Kōe, Yokota Kisaburō, and Suzuki Takeo in Suzuki (1977, pp. 622–625).
2. "Article 38 (1), Statute of the International Court of Justice." The current Statute lists a fourth source, "judicial decisions and the teachings of the most highly qualified publicists" but only as a subsidiary means.
3. Tanaka added that "naturally, the general principles of law are distinguishable from natural law. However, natural law occupies an important part of this precept" (Tanaka 1971a, p. 21).
4. See Uemura (2002), Uemura and Kaneko (2007), Takahashi (2015–2016).
5. See for example, Hall (2001) and Subramanya (2007).
6. See Takeshita (2013).
7. In addition to the many articles by Arata Shin'ichirō discussed above in Chapter 4, see Funase (2009).

References

Article 38 (1), Statute of the International Court of Justice. https://www.icj-cij.org/en/statute#CHAPTER_II. Accessed 8 August 2018.

Funase, Hajime. 2009. Tanaka Kōtarō no kōtō kyōiku ron to sono shisōshi-teki ichi ni tsuite. *Hisutoria* 213 (January): 253–278.

Hall, Stephen. 2001. The Persistent Spectre: Natural Law, International Order and the Limits of Legal Positivism. *European Journal of International Law* 12 (2): 269–307.

Koga, Katsujiro. 2014. *Kagami no kindai: "hō no shihai"o meguru nihon to chūgoku*. Tokyo: Shunjū Sha.

Shibasaki, Atsushi. 2010. Christianity and the Making of a Modern Worldview in Japan: International Thought of Tanaka Kotaro (1890–1974). *Journal of Global Media Studies* 7: 31–40.

Subramanya, T.R. 2007. The Universal Declaration of Human Rights at 59. In *World Constitutionalism*, ed. Anthony D'Souza. Newcastle, UK: Cambridge Scholars.

Suzuki, Takeo (ed.). 1977. *Tanaka Kōtarō: hito to gyōseki*. Tokyo: Yūhikaku.

Takahashi, Eiji. 2015–2016. 'Reception' and 'Convergence' of Japanese and German Corporate Law. *University of St. Thomas Law Journal* 12: 228–248.

Takamine, Sadako. 1974. Rakujitsu no kagayaki: Tanaka Kōtarō sensei no omoide—kirisutosha to seiji. *Koe* (July); reprinted in Suzuki Takeo ed., *Tanaka Kōtarō: hito to gyōseki*. Tokyo: Yūhikaku, 458–462.

Takeshita, Keisuke. 2013. Sadajiro Atobe and Kotaro Tanaka: The Universal Private International Law School of Thought in Japan. *Japanese Yearbook of International Law* 56: 217–242.

Tanaka, Kōtarō. 1961. *Watakushi no rirekisho*. Tokyo: Shunjū Sha.

———. 1970. Bummei to dōtoku. *Kokoro* 23 (6): 2–9.

———. 1971a. The Character of World Law in the International Court of Justice. *The Japanese Annual of International Law* 15: 1–22.

———. 1971b. Zagurebbu. *Kokoro* 24 (November): 389–390.

———. 1972. Some Observations on Peace, Law, and Human Rights. In *Transnational Law in a Changing Society: Essays in Honor of Philip C. Jessup*, ed. Wolfgang Friedmann, Louis Henkin, and Oliver Lissitzyn. New York and London: Columbia University.

Uemura, Tatsuo. 2002. *Kaisha hō kaikaku: kōkai kabushiki kaisha hō no kōsō*. Tokyo: Iwanami Shoten.

Uemura, Tatsuo, and Akira Kaneko. 2007. *Kabushiki kaisha wa doko e iku no ka*. Tokyo: Nihon Keizai Shimbun Shuppan Sha.

List of Publications by Tanaka Kōtarō in Western Languages

"Fonction de la coutume en droit commercial." *Recueil d'etudes sur les sources du droit en l'honneur de François Gény* (Paris, 1934): pp. 247–256.

Caratteristiche del contratto di assicurazione, Number 3 (Roma: Istituto Nazionale della Assicurazioni Anno III, 1936).

"L'influence des idées occidentales sur le Japon." *Nova et Vetera*, Volume XI, Number 3 (July–September 1936): pp. 300–306.

"Nature giuridica dei rapporti cambiari." *Rivista del Diritto Commerciale*, Number 9 et 10 (Anno XXXIV, 1936).

Fonti del diritto commerciale (Roma: Padova, CEDAM, 1936).

"Il Diritto et la Technica." *Rivista Internazionale di Filosofia del Diritto* (1936).

"La divisione del lavoro e la responsabilità civile nel diritto commerciale." *Il Foro Italiano*, Volume 61 (1936): pp. 219–226.

"Critique de la science juridique pure chez Kelsen, sa negation du droit naturel et son relativisme philosophique." *Acta Congressus iuridici internationalis*, Volume 5 (1937): pp. 419–426.

"Idée du droit mondial." *Annales de l'Institut de Droit Comparé de l'Université de Paris*, Volume III (1938): pp. 303–315.

"La méthode du droit commercial." *Recueil d'études en l'honneur d'Edouard Lambert* (Paris: Recueil Sirey, 1938): pp. 477–485.

"Liberalism as a Japanese Problem." *Japan To-Day* (June 1, 1938); reprinted in Sadami Suzuki ed., *Japan To-Day: Bungeishunju's European Language War-Time Propaganda* (Kyoto, Japan: International Research Center for Japanese Studies, 2011): pp. 119–121.

K. M. Doak, *Tanaka Kōtarō and World Law*, Global Political Thinkers,
https://doi.org/10.1007/978-3-030-02035-4

"Cured of Relativism." In Severin and Stephen Lamping, O.F.M., trans. and eds., *Through Hundred Gates* (Milwaukee, WI: The Bruce Publishing Company, 1939): pp. 260–264.

El Internacionalismo y la idea del derecho natural en Savigny (Buenos Aires: Sección Publicaciones del Seminario de Ciencias Jurídicas y Sociales, 1939).

"The Ideological Basis of the U.N.: Difference Between It and The League." *Nippon Times*, Wednesday (May 29, 1946): p. 4.

"Theodor Sternberg." *Revista Internazionale di Filosofia del Diritto*, 1950 Fasc. III–IV.

"In Search of Truth and Peace." In Ryusaku Tsunoda, Wm. Theodore de Bary and Donald Keene, eds., *Sources of Japanese Tradition*, Volume II (New York: Columbia University Press, 2005): pp. 1077–1081. Except from Tanaka, *Shinri to heiwa o motomete* (1949).

"MacArthur and Japan." *Nippon Times*, Friday (April 27, 1951): p. 6.

"The Present Crisis of Japanese Education." *Contemporary Japan* (1951): pp. 5–14.

"Peace and Justice." *Nippon Times* (January 17, 1952). Reprinted in *Catholic University Law Review*, Volume 70 (1951): pp. 70–74.

"Peace and Justice: Japan's Place in the Family of Nations." *American Bar Association Journal*, Volume 38 (August 1952): pp. 663–664, 675.

"The Democratization of the Japanese Administration of Justice." In *Japan's Problems* (Tokyo: Ministry of Foreign Affairs, Public Information and Cultural Affairs, 1953): pp. 1–14.

"A Sketch of a Theory of World Law." Source unknown (1954): pp. 1–15.

"What Is Necessary to Make Democracy Work in Japan." *The Free China Review*, Volume V, Number 6 (June 1955): pp. 15–18.

"Educational Values from the Viewpoint of Integral Humanism." *Missionary Bulletin*, Volume XI, Number 8 (October 1957): pp. 627–631; Volume XI, Number 9 (November 1957): pp. 696–702.

"Democracy and Judicial Administration in Japan." *J. Int'l Comm. Jur.* 7 (1959): pp. 7–19.

"The Rule of Law and the Natural Law." *USAF JAG Bull. 6*, Volume II, Number 5 (1960): pp. 6–8.

"The Theory of the Fundamental Law of Education." *Journal of Social and Political Ideas in Japan*, Volume 1, Number 3 (December 1963): pp. 33–36.

"Japanese Law." In Arthur Larson and C. Wilfred Jenks, et al., eds., *Sovereignty Within the Law* (London: Sevens and Sons, 1965): pp. 223–241.

"The Character of World Law in the International Court of Justice." *The Japanese Annual of International Law*, Number 15 (1971): pp. 1–22.

"Some Observations on Peace, Law, and Human Rights." In Wolfgang Friedmann, Louis Henkin and Oliver Lissitzyn, eds., *Transnational Law in a Changing Society: Essays in Honor of Philip C. Jessup* (New York and London: Columbia University Press, 1972): pp. 242–256.

Index

K. M. Doak, *Tanaka Kōtarō and World Law*, Global Political Thinkers,
https://doi.org/10.1007/978-3-030-02035-4

The manufacturer's authorised representative in the EU is Springer Nature Customer Service Centre GmbH, Europaplatz 3, 69115 Heidelberg, Germany. If you have any concerns regarding our products, please contact ProductSafety@springernature.com

Printed and bound by CPI Group (UK) Ltd, Croydon, CR0 4YY
30/09/2026
02225666-0008